M000159582

DISASTER RECOVERY, CRISIS RESPONSE, AND BUSINESS CONTINUITY

A MANAGEMENT DESK REFERENCE

Jamie Watters

Apress·

Disaster Recovery, Crisis Response, and Business Continuity: A Management Desk Reference

Copyright © 2014 by Jamie Watters

This work is subject to copyright. All rights are reserved by the Publisher, whether the whole or part of the material is concerned, specifically the rights of translation, reprinting, reuse of illustrations, recitation, broadcasting, reproduction on microfilms or in any other physical way, and transmission or information storage and retrieval, electronic adaptation, computer software, or by similar or dissimilar methodology now known or hereafter developed. Exempted from this legal reservation are brief excerpts in connection with reviews or scholarly analysis or material supplied specifically for the purpose of being entered and executed on a computer system, for exclusive use by the purchaser of the work. Duplication of this publication or parts thereof is permitted only under the provisions of the Copyright Law of the Publisher's location, in its current version, and permission for use must always be obtained from Springer. Permissions for use may be obtained through RightsLink at the Copyright Clearance Center. Violations are liable to prosecution under the respective Copyright Law.

ISBN-13 (pbk): 978-1-4302-6406-4

ISBN-13 (electronic): 978-1-4302-6407-1

Trademarked names, logos, and images may appear in this book. Rather than use a trademark symbol with every occurrence of a trademarked name, logo, or image we use the names, logos, and images only in an editorial fashion and to the benefit of the trademark owner, with no intention of infringement of the trademark.

The use in this publication of trade names, trademarks, service marks, and similar terms, even if they are not identified as such, is not to be taken as an expression of opinion as to whether or not they are subject to proprietary rights.

While the advice and information in this book are believed to be true and accurate at the date of publication, neither the authors nor the editors nor the publisher can accept any legal responsibility for any errors or omissions that may be made. The publisher makes no warranty, express or implied, with respect to the material contained herein.

President and Publisher: Paul Manning
Acquisitions Editor: Jeff Olson
Editorial Board: Steve Anglin, Mark Beckner, Ewan Buckingham, Gary Cornell, Louise Corrigan, James DeWolf, Jonathan Gennick, Jonathan Hassell, Robert Hutchinson, Michelle Lowman, James Markham, Matthew Moodie, Jeff Olson, Jeffrey Pepper, Douglas Pundick,
Ben Renow-Clarke, Dominic Shakeshaft, Gwenan Spearing, Matt Wade, Steve Weiss, Tom Welsh
Coordinating Editor: Kevin Shea
Copy Editors: Kim Wimpsett and Mary Bearden
Compositor: SPi Global
Indexer: SPi Global
Cover Designer: Anna Ishchenko

Distributed to the book trade worldwide by Springer Science+Business Media New York, 233 Spring Street, 6th Floor, New York, NY 10013. Phone 1-800-SPRINGER, fax (201) 348-4505, e-mail orders-ny@springer-sbm.com, or visit www.springeronline.com. Apress Media, LLC is a California LLC and the sole member (owner) is Springer Science + Business Media Finance Inc (SSBM Finance Inc). SSBM Finance Inc is a Delaware corporation.

For information on translations, please e-mail rights@apress.com, or visit www.apress.com.

Apress and friends of ED books may be purchased in bulk for academic, corporate, or promotional use. eBook versions and licenses are also available for most titles. For more information, reference our Special Bulk Sales–eBook Licensing web page at www.apress.com/bulk-sales.

Any source code or other supplementary materials referenced by the author in this text is available to readers at www.apress.com. For detailed information about how to locate your book's source code, go to www.apress.com/source-code/.

Apress Business: The Unbiased Source of Business Information

Apress business books provide essential information and practical advice, each written for practitioners by recognized experts. Busy managers and professionals in all areas of the business world—and at all levels of technical sophistication—look to our books for the actionable ideas and tools they need to solve problems, update and enhance their professional skills, make their work lives easier, and capitalize on opportunity.

Whatever the topic on the business spectrum—entrepreneurship, finance, sales, marketing, management, regulation, information technology, among others—Apress has been praised for providing the objective information and unbiased advice you need to excel in your daily work life. Our authors have no axes to grind; they understand they have one job only—to deliver up-to-date, accurate information simply, concisely, and with deep insight that addresses the real needs of our readers.

It is increasingly hard to find information—whether in the news media, on the Internet, and now all too often in books—that is even-handed and has your best interests at heart. We therefore hope that you enjoy this book, which has been carefully crafted to meet our standards of quality and unbiased coverage.

We are always interested in your feedback or ideas for new titles. Perhaps you'd even like to write a book yourself. Whatever the case, reach out to us at editorial@apress.com and an editor will respond swiftly. Incidentally, at the back of this book, you will find a list of useful related titles. Please visit us at www.apress.com to sign up for newsletters and discounts on future purchases.

The Apress Business Team

For Ray Trapnell

Contents

About the Author

Jamie Watters has worked in business continuity since 1985. He has seen the field of IT disaster recovery (DR) mature into service continuity and give birth to the related discipline of business continuity. As a leading practitioner, he has innovated in the fields of business continuity, crisis management, work area recovery, and DR. Jamie has set up and run the business continuity and DR programs for leading financial services firms, including Barclays, HSBC, Santander, Nationwide, and Capital One. He has also worked in other sectors, including airlines, retail, wholesale, IT, and consultancy. He is currently the Global BCM Program Manager for Global Banking & Markets at HSBC. He has hands-on experience running BCM programs in all continents except Antarctica.

Acknowledgments

I would like to thank a few people. First, I have to thank my wife, Janet—for her patience—and my three children, Libby, Freya, and Ben, who brought me the happiness that comes from giving and not getting. Thanks also to my dad, Doug, for making me a better person and my father-in-law, John, for being himself and for always being there even though he's in Turkey. Special thanks go to Jeff Olson at Apress for finding me, having faith and patience in me, and bringing much needed style and rigor to the text.

Finally, I'd like to thank all the colleagues and friends who have helped with their council, insight, wise words, criticism, innovation, and good practice over the years, in particular: Kamlesh Parmar, Ian Francis, Paul Cowan, Kerrie Smith, David Thompson, Nick Simms, Howard Goodman, Raghu Tellaprapragada, William Fawcett, Karen Woodward, Nigel Fenton, Adele Lock, Scott Westwood, Rachel Low, Bob Piggott, Martin Byrne, Andy Todd, Soterios Papayiannis, Karen Azzopardi, Cath Stringer, Ray Trapnell, Richard Bridgford, Tim Armit, Andy Tomkinson, John Tucker, Mark Liddington, Keith Tilley, Mike Osborne, Tim Chadwick, Julia Graham, Luke Bazzard, Lee Webb, Vicki Gavin, Andrew McCracken, Linda Hall, Chris Keeling, David Shaw, Jeremy Burns, Paul Ingham, Pele Johnson, Keith Oldham, Mark Dignum, Dan Bridge, Peter Lightfoot, Andy Young, Andy Gower, Richard Fisher, Neil Simmonite, Scott Moseley, and Howard D'Silva.

.

Introduction

Business continuity and disaster recovery have emerged as critical aspects of business planning in the past few years. It was born in high-risk and highly regulated industries but is now spreading rapidly into all sectors and every type of organization. Why? More and more businesses are affected by natural and manmade disasters, more regulators expect to see recovery plans in place for industries beyond health and finance, more organizations expect to see continuity policies in place at vendor sites, and insurers drop rates for businesses showing greater awareness of security protocols. More important, in the age of 24/7 business, customers expect to be able to do business with you when it's convenient for them. Never mind that your city just flooded; just send me my goods or complete my transaction.

Originally, business continuity and recovery planning were the domain of a few elite consultants. Historically, consultants charged a premium for their skills and knowledge to organizations. These companies had no choice but to pay for custom consultancy engagements. Now, with increased need for continuity planning and more practitioners embedded inside organizations, business continuity has effectively been commoditized—every business needs to plan for unexpected events or pay the consequences. This commoditization is a good thing because organizations need continuity plans in place quickly, at the lowest cost and with the least pain.

This book covers the key aspects of business continuity and disaster recovery. It is written so anyone can pick it up, read it, then go and do it. It tells you what you need to do, gives you simple tools to use, and tells you what questions you need to ask and from whom you should seek the answers. Just as important, it provides checklists and templates that will help you put a credible plan in quick order.

Why Read This Book?

You have a job to do protecting your company from disasters, hackers, supply problems, and anything else that might keep you from fulfilling your mission. I want you to learn from my mistakes and quickly acquire the necessary knowledge to get the job done. I want you to avoid the trial-and-error journey that my peers and I had to suffer as we learned the hard way.

So if you want to learn all the essential aspects of business continuity while avoiding the pain, then this book is for you.

There are lots of excellent books that tell you what you've got to do. This book is for people who want to know how to do it.

The aim of this book is to explain (in simple terms) all the key elements of business continuity and disaster recovery for people who need to:

- Learn the basics of business continuity fast

- Get something in place today so they'll have a chance if disaster strikes tomorrow

- Avoid the principal mistakes people in your position often make

- Prepare solid plans that people find easy to use and maintain

- Identify and fix security and continuity gaps in your systems, processes, or people

- Test your continuity plans and the people, suppliers, and technology that your organization depends on

- Make sure your staff knows what to expect from the organization if disaster strikes—and what the organization should expect from you

- Become compliant with the demands of internal auditors, external regulators, and business partners that expect them to have solid, demonstrable continuity plans in place

- Extend the principles of continuity into supplier organizations and business partners so that third parties are able to meet your needs

- Keep all the plans, scripts, solutions, and other functions up to date without making it into a full-time job

If it's your job to accomplish any of these things, read on. This book is for you!

Who Should Read This Book

This book is relevant to anyone who is in anyway involved in business continuity, crisis management, and disaster recovery (DR).

This list includes:

- Business continuity managers

- Business continuity coordinators—people who look after local plans and do the day-to-day administration and testing for their department

- IT staff and technicians who support business continuity or DR solutions and are involved in testing or have responsibility for some element of the recovery of their business

- IT architects and developers who are responsible for including resilience into their designs and the solutions they deliver

- Executives accountable for the continued smooth running of their businesses, funding business continuity efforts, and making sure it meets underlying business needs

- Staff who have a role to play in preparing plans, testing, or have responsibilities in disaster recovery situation

- Auditors who are responsible for making sure that the organization's continuity arrangements meet business needs

- Suppliers that need to meet their customers' needs in regard to business continuity and DR

- Suppliers that sell business continuity or DR services

Practices to Underpin Frameworks

There are many excellent business continuity management (BCM) frameworks. BS25999[1] and AS/NZS 5050[2] are two good examples. Each sets out what you have to do and to some extent what you should learn. They also provide a common vocabulary for you to use. The problem with standards and frameworks, however, is that in general they don't tell you how to do anything. How do you assess a business impact analysis? How do you plan and deliver a DR test? How do you keep your staff informed? How do you keep your plans updated?

---

[1] http://en.wikipedia.org/wiki/BS_25999
[2] http://en.wikipedia.org/wiki/Business_continuity

In this book, I mean to plug such gaps by sharing my experience and describing what I and other experienced BC/DR people actually do.

For some people, BCM is an emotive subject; many practitioners are exacting and fussy in what they do. To be frank, I'm not overly attached to what we do. Continuity planning is simply something that must be done in our day and age. But I do care about getting results efficiently and effectively. I also like to do that without upsetting or distracting too many other people! But it's possible to get bogged down in detail and perfectionism. To avoid that, do what I do and keep your mind on the practical.

For this reason, if you read anything in this book and can think of a better way of doing things, don't think badly about me. Instead think, "I should send this idea to Jamie!"[3] Take the time to gather your thoughts and let me know so I can improve what I do and then improve this book!

Why Listen to Me?

First, I've spent most of the past 25 years working in business continuity and IT disaster recovery–related roles, much of it in the financial services and banking industry, and should have learned most of what there is to know.

So, what I'm offering you is the chance to exploit my mistakes and gain my insight in days—not months or years!

One of the key issues I've faced, and an issue that will probably concern you too, is how to deliver business continuity through people who have other full-time roles that have nothing to do with business continuity—people for whom business continuity is a pain and a distraction from their main role. If that describes you, you've come to the right book. My overarching goal is to make your job easier, something I can do by telling you how things play out in the real world.

When creating a business continuity program, I've also come to realize it's essential to build it with the following principle in mind:

> The program must address the deeper technical issues but without needing full-time experts to make it work.

In short, I believe my job is to make business continuity simple and suitable for people who only look at their business continuity/DR plans once or twice a year. So wherever possible I will aim to demystify business continuity, so that when people come back to their plans nine months down the line, it'll be fairly easy to understand or implement. If you want to learn to make it simple, then I'm your man.

---

[3]Reach me through www.bcmdeskreference.com/

Structure of the Book

The chapters are written so that you can either dip in as you need to or you can read it section by section. The sections are organized as you should ideally approach business continuity, so unless you have a specific need it's best to read the book in chapter order.

However, if sections or chapters don't apply—for example, you don't have any third-parties contractors—you might want to skip them.

I've tried to highlight the relevance of each chapter at the beginning so you can decide in a few moments if it's worth reading on.

The book is organized in the following five parts:

- **Part One: Introduction to Business Continuity and Disaster Recovery**. Introduces the basic concepts and provides you with the who, what, when, where—and a high-level how—of business continuity, crisis management, and disaster recovery.

- **Part Two: Plan for Business Continuity and Disaster Recovery**. Explains how to plan for business continuity. The section looks at both business continuity plans and IT disaster recovery plans.

- **Part Three: Test and Maintain Your Continuity and Recovery Plans**. Examines all the testing and maintenance that is relevant to business continuity with chapters on IT testing, business testing, and maintenance.

- **Part Four: Execute the Plan**. There's no point in having plans and solutions if you can't deploy them at a time of crisis. This section explains what you need to do to make sure you steer your organization though whatever disruption comes your way. More than that, it also covers the return from contingency to normal operations.

- **Part Five: Appendices**. Here you'll find copies of useful things like checklists, templates, and processes that I describe in the book. You can use them to get your own business continuity up and running. The appendices also include some useful reference information and links to other useful resources.

Let's get started!

Introduction to Business Continuity and Disaster Recovery

Business Continuity Management

An Overview

In this chapter we introduce the key concepts of business continuity, explain how an organization should approach business continuity, and explore the roles that underpin business continuity. Everything covered here will be quite high level, and all the key themes will be explored in more detail in the subsequent chapters.

What Is Business Continuity Management?

Business continuity management (BCM) exists to avoid any interruptions that could lead to either significant losses or a failure to achieve the organization's principal objectives. BCM is both a process and a discipline.

The sorts of things business continuity exists to deal with are wide ranging, from the mundane to the most dramatic events, such as from someone leaving the water running to volcanic ash clouds or space weather. The aims of business continuity vary depending on the nature of the organization and are as general as keeping the light on and as specific as providing all staff with chargers so that they can use their phones and laptops following a Superstorm Sandy–type event.

Business continuity is an umbrella discipline and encompasses some specific disciplines such as business continuity planning, where you do all the work to prepare for a disaster; service continuity, where you set up, maintain, and test the technology solutions that support business continuity; and crisis management, which is the process you will use to respond to major events that your "business as usual" processes can't cope with.

KEY POINTS OF THE CHAPTER

This chapter is basic grounding and is relevant for everyone. It does the following:

- Explains why we have business continuity

- Describes how business continuity is delivered

- Introduces some basic concepts and vocabulary

- Introduces the key roles for people involved

- Outlines some key standards for business continuity and disaster recovery (DR)

- Identifies further sources of reference, services, and support

Business Continuity as a Process

The process of business continuity, also known as the *business continuity life cycle*, describes how any organization should go about ensuring that critical activities are performed no matter what else is happening.

The process is cyclical and follows the same basic steps as most processes of continuous improvement (Figure 1-1).

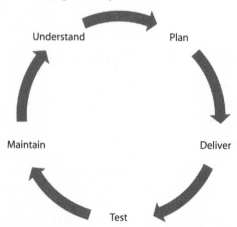

Figure 1-1. Business continuity life cycle

The process is first about understanding what constitutes a critical process, then plans how it will be introduced, then designs and delivers supporting solutions, then tests it all, and then is maintained. The cycle repeats itself *ad infinitum*.

Business continuity as a process really means that it is repeatable and can be undertaken by a wide range of people, with different levels of experience and seniority, and yet can achieve consistent high-quality results. Process is important because it gives people something they can do, and it has the added benefit of making everything auditable, which is increasingly important.

Business Continuity as a Discipline

When I talk about BCM as a discipline, I'm talking about how the tasks connect with the people who will do them. The discipline of business continuity comprises policies and the collection of people and teams in your organization that are responsible for the various steps that make up the business continuity life cycle and making sure all remain in good working order. Business continuity people are also responsible for monitoring incidents so that in the event of a business interruption the plans to ensure continuity get invoked as quickly as possible.

Typically, people supporting continuity include the following:

- Continuity planners, who identify what is critical and decide how it can be continued through an interruption.

- IT service continuity professionals, who are responsible for making sure the critical IT services are available to support critical business activities.

- Crisis management team, which is responsible for monitoring the business for potential interruption events and then making sure that timely action is taken, which would normally involve invoking the business continuity plans and recovering any required IT services.

How Is Business Continuity Implemented?

Exactly how business continuity is implemented depends on your organization. The details have to make sense to the people who will use it. What constitutes a policy in one organization will be different from another.

Ideally you should have the following:

- A policy that sets out what is expected in terms of business continuity

- A defined process that says how the organization will achieve business continuity

- A set of tools and templates that can be used by people following the process to ensure consistent and high-quality results

- Someone who is accountable for making sure that business continuity is in place and effective

- An ongoing business continuity program that manages all the activities that make up the process, checks on quality, promotes awareness, and identifies issues and escalates them for action

- A set of people who have clear responsibility for the activities that relate to business continuity

There may be other things that make sense, and the details need to be consistent with how you do things in your organization and line up with any related processes, such as how you escalate issues.

Criticality

Criticality is how we rank things by importance to the organization. You can think of it as a line, and how many times you divide the lineup depends on your organization and its appetite for risks. Criticality is a key concept in business continuity management that needs further explanation.

Fundamentally, business continuity is driven by an understanding of what's critical and how that criticality changes over time.

Broadly speaking, activities can be divided into the following categories:

- *Mission critical:* The few things you have to do if your business is to survive

- *Essential:* The things you must do that will cause a massive, but not immediately fatal, impact if they are not done

- *Important:* The things to do after you've taken care of the previous two

- *Not important:* Things you can put on the back burner during the disaster

For example, in a bank, settlement is life and death and so fits in the first category. If the bank fails to settle, the whole financial system can fail. For the same bank, servicing customer accounts is important, but if not done for 24 hours, the impact is not fatal to the bank. However, you may find that a point comes when the backlog builds up to a point that it can't be cleared faster than new work comes in. At this point, it becomes critical. Selling new products is deemed least important and can be suspended in order that available resources can be directed to looking after existing customers or other more critical activities.

Of course, it's never as simple as that because things that are not life and death in the first 24 hours may become so if they are not performed within, say, 2 days.

Note   It's essential that criticality is defined in clear terms and that these terms are adopted by all areas concerned. See Appendix A for an example of criticality levels. These are not universal; you will need to tailor them to reflect your organization's priorities.

Severity Levels

If criticality levels provide a measure of how important something is to the business, severity levels tell us how significant events are.

To understand these differences, imagine criticality is how deep you are cut, and severity is where you're being cut. So, you might cut your arm off and live, but cut your head off and you're dead.

For an example of severity levels, see Appendix K.

Note   For an illustration of how severity levels can be mapped to criticalities, look at Appendix L.

Scenarios and Risks

Some events have an impact on your business. It could be a fire, a flood, a power outage, or what have you. Consequently, you need some activity to recover or manage the impact. The action should either address the issue or maintain the delivery of your service. If you manage the event properly, you can recover without much fallout. Of course, if you don't manage the impact, it can lead to disaster!

Figure 1-2 depicts the life cycle of a disaster.

Figure 1-2. Life cycle of a disaster

Focus on Outcomes, Not Causes

A major mistake many professionals make is to focus on the possible causes of events. The problem is that there are infinite possible causes. A real risk is that you can spend all your life doing risk assessments and are not ready for what comes along.

A better approach is to focus on the impacts and how they manifest themselves in terms of outcomes. It makes much more sense to do this because, for an infinite number of potential causes, the possible impacts boil down into only five outcome scenarios.

That means you focus first on preparing the basic elements of business continuity so that you can survive the five possible outcome scenarios.

■ **Tip** Don't spend any time trying to identify all the possible potential causes of a problem and preparing for each one in turn. Instead, focus on preparing for the possible outcomes.

Once you're prepared for the scenarios, then you can think increasingly about mitigating the likely causes!

MAXIMIZE YOUR TIME AT THE START

In a less than a day you can have the basics of a plan that will enable you to avoid most potential disasters. Or you can spend months on risk assessment and impact analysis only to face a disaster before you've even started on the basics of a plan.

This is quite contentious, and many "experts" disagree with me and advocate a methodical approach where you work through all the steps sequentially and complete detailed analysis first. I wonder if they are more attached to their methods than the goal, which is to make sure we and our businesses survive no matter what!

The Five Possible Outcome Scenarios

As mentioned, there are infinite possible causes or risks to your business, but they manifest as one of just five possible outcomes. The potential scenarios are as follows:

- *Loss of technology*: The technology you use is not available or doesn't work.

- *Loss of a building*: A building is destroyed or out of action for the medium to long term.

- *Denial of access to a building*: Your staff is not allowed into their place of work.

- *Loss of staff*: Key staff members are unable to attend work.

- *Loss of a supplier*: A supplier is unable to provide critical services, products, or resources.

Business continuity is all about preparing for and ultimately managing the responses to these scenarios. It's important to take a risk-based approach to potential outcomes based on your unique situation. For example, you will want to focus first on the most likely scenario for your organization and those solutions or elements of business continuity that will maximize your chances of survival (the first level on your criticality list). For one company it might be technology recovery; for another, it might be continuing critical activities such as fulfilling orders.

Let's look at each of the five scenarios in more detail.

Responding to Loss of Technology

IT systems are probably the most common cause of a business interruption. Hence, the backbone of your business continuity may be your strategy for ensuring the continuity of critical systems.

Normally, you'd have an alternative system that can be used. Ideally, it will be located at a secondary site that has independent infrastructure, such as a site with power that is far enough away to be unaffected by the event affecting the main site.

If the criticality of the function demands that you cannot tolerate even a brief outage, you need to consider investing in additional resiliency so that the system can continue operating even if its major components are disrupted or there's a local infrastructure failure.

Chapter 5 has a fuller explanation of DR and resiliency.

For non-IT technology such as machinery, you should consider suitable strategies, such as having backup equipment or, if practical, the ability to switch to an external supplier to serve your critical needs.

Responding to Loss of a Building

If a building is destroyed or out of action for the medium to long term, say by a severe fire or hurricane, you'll need some way of continuing any required activities that are normally completed at that location.

Ideally you will have either of the following:

- A secondary location where key workers can go to resume critical activities
- The ability to switch the work to another, unaffected location where the work can be completed

We normally call the secondary site option work area recovery (WAR). WAR can be provided either in-house, where you have some spare capacity in another building, or by a third-party vendor.

Ultimately, you will also need to find somewhere or some way to get the less critical activities done because few of them will be deferrable indefinitely.

I will deal with WAR and other strategies fully in Chapter 6.

Responding to Denial of Access to a Building

More likely than actually losing your building is that you find that your staff members are not allowed into their place of work because of a local event. This might be a fire, flood, utilities outage, and so on. In many cases, these events will be minor or not directly affect the integrity of your building.

This is likely to be short term; such events often last less than 24 hours. Because of the short nature, it's critical that you gauge the impact quickly and estimate likely resolution time. It's not unreasonable to have staff waiting for an hour, but a day could be disastrous.

If the outage is longer than one day, you will probably treat it in exactly the same way you would if you had lost the building.

Responding to Loss of Staff

Another possibility is that your staff is unable or unwilling to get to work.

At the extreme, this could be because a significant percentage is incapacitated—say by an epidemic—but it also addresses the more likely possibility that your staff can't get to work because of transport or the weather. Another possibility is that people are unwilling to come to work because of industrial action, because of fear of being infected, or because they have more pressing commitments at home.

This is the most difficult scenario to deal with because it comes in a wide variety of flavors, can strike anywhere, and can scale from a localized event up to a global one.

To cope, you first need a good understanding of critical activities, the skills required to complete these activities, and exactly which people would be required to keep operations running. Armed with this information, you can start to do some preventative work such as the cross training of staff where single points of failure exist. A single point of failure is, for example, where you depend on a single person in a single location to perform a critical task.

Responding to Loss of a Supplier

As the majority of organizations remain focused on their core activities and outsource their noncore activities, they have become increasingly dependent on their supply chains.

Consequently, to achieve business continuity, you need to understand these dependencies.

Understanding alone is not enough. You'll also need to be aware of any problems that may occur in your supply chain so that at the first sign of trouble you can secure an alternative supply. In some instances, this may involve insourcing the activity. Whatever your strategy, if problems are appearing on the horizon, you must make sure that the supplier is managing its response effectively. If not, then you must be prepared to act swiftly.

I'd stress the need for "management by exception" here. You really don't want to be monitoring every business as usual activity. What you need is to be included in any incident escalation and reporting, and you need to make sure that this communication is swift and unimpeded.

■ **Tip**   Rather than keeping a watchful eye on suppliers for potential trouble, ask suppliers to keep you informed of incidents and ensure lines of communication are clear. You will, of course, want to watch for clues that trouble is brewing—financial problems, labor issues, and so on.

Each year, you have to do more work with less time, money, and resources to get it done. The great lesson from this is that you have to invest time up front, in things such as good incident escalation, that work without you so that you are freed from day-to-day involvement until it becomes necessary.

The Importance of Time

Already we've started to discuss some requirements of maintaining business continuity: identifying critical tasks, critical people, and any critical resources that are needed to do these tasks.

But the common denominator for everything in business continuity is time.

From an IT point of view, for example, business continuity requirements are some of your most important nonfunctional requirements (NFRs) when you are delivering IT solutions.

Broadly speaking, these requirements can be framed as follows:

- You need to know how long you can survive without doing something or having something happen.

- You need to know how long operations can be sustained in a reduced capacity.

- You need to know how much of the work you can afford to lose before it proves disastrous, as opposed to how much you can afford to lose before it merely causes inconvenience. Again, this is measured in time. For example, you might decide you can afford to lose no more than two hours of work.

In business continuity, the time-based requirements have been defined as a set of objectives. We will look at these next.

Recovery Time Objective

The *recovery time objective* (RTO) defines how quickly a system or process must be recovered after it fails.

Criticality is normally closely associated with RTOs. So, your most critical processes might have an RTO of 0. In other words, you can't tolerate any downtime. The next level might be 0 to 2 hours, and so on.

There's a lot of debate about RTO. Quite often, people inside the same organization may have very different views of how an RTO is defined. For example, the business will mean exactly what I just said—that RTO represents the time from an event occurring until the system, service, or facility is restored. However, in the same organization, the IT department might take RTO to mean how quickly the system will be brought up after the decision is made to start the recovery.

To understand the issues, consider the following scenario. It might take IT 3 hours to bring a system up, plus 30 minutes for the business to set it up. The business may have identified a need to get the system back in 4 hours. Sounds OK: 3 hours + 30 minutes is less than 4 hours, right? But, this doesn't allow for "management" time to identify the issue, assess it, decide on which action to take, and perhaps notify decision makers and get authorization.

In practice, it might be 3 hours before IT starts the recovery! From their point of view, they are fine with that because they still meet their version of the RTO, taking 3 hours to recover and adding on the 30 minutes set up. Yet it has now taken 6 hours and 30 minutes. So, while IT may think it met the RTO, the business has lost $2 million!

For this reason, I recommend you split the overall business recovery time from the system recovery time. To this end, I'll introduce another term, *maximum disruption time* (MDT), which is starting to be used more widely.

Maximum Disruption Time

MDTs are used to define the business's overall recovery objective, that is, the time from an event occurring until the system is available again.

I recommend using it for the overall business RTO rather than IT's because the IT RTO will probably be embedded in far more reports and used more widely than the business one. However, it does mean that if you are introducing MTDs, you will have to change all your reporting.

The MDT gives the people managing an event the broader context. Given the MTD and the RTO for the systems, they can see how much time they can spend trying to fix the problem before they begin the recovery.

There are different terms used in different organizations, but the most common one used as an alternative to MTD is *maximum allowable downtime* (MAD).

Maximum Tolerable Period of Disruption

As if this wasn't confusing enough, recent standards have proposed that we should also have a measure of how long it is before an interruption causes the complete failure of an organization, the *maximum tolerable period of disruption* (MTPoD). This makes some sense, but in practice it doesn't seem to be widely understood or adopted.

Tip If you can shape the life cycle, I recommend you stick with RTO for IT and MDT for the business.

Recovery Point Objective

Recovery point objective (RPO) defines the maximum amount of data loss you can tolerate. In other words, the RPO tells you how far back you can revert your data when you are recovering a system or process.

This has major implications for IT because it dictates how frequently data backups must be made and dictates the architecture of the system itself. These two things have a significant impact on development, testing, maintenance, and consequently costs.

In simple terms, if a system fails (say it goes down at 1:00 p.m.), the RPO defines how far back it's acceptable to roll the data. In this example, it might be acceptable to go back to start of day. Now if the working day is 8 hours, you would set RPO to 8 hours. Conversely, it might be a banking system where it's unacceptable to lose any transactional data, and you'll set the RPO at 0.

In practical terms, an RPO of 0 is not guaranteed because, at the point of failure, transactions can be lost, but the loss will be at a manageable level—a small number of transactions rather than thousands or millions.

Who Does What?

Now that you understand the importance of time in business continuity management, let's look at the roles people take. I've summarized the key roles in sections, each of which sets out what it is that they are supposed to achieve, the specific tasks they undertake, and the outputs or deliverables they should produce.[1]

Role: Business Continuity Manager

Objective: Ensure that business continuity is in place and the organization has a proven ability to recover.

---

[1] I've included a type of RACI matrix in Appendix B, which defines the key roles in terms of accountability (where the buck stops), responsibility (who actually does it), consultation (who should be involved in discussions), and communication (who must be informed about it). RACI (which stands for Responsible, Accountable, Contributing, and Informed) is used widely, and I've added my own innovation by adding an extra dimension to the RACI so that it also includes oversight. Hence, I've called it a CAIRO diagram.

Tasks:

- Set policy.
- Create BCM process.
- Provide business continuity tools.
- Implement BCM process.
- Ensure staff is aware of duties.
- Assess the maturity and quality of BCM and report issues and risks.
- Ensure the business continuity solutions and plans are tested.

Deliverables:

- Policy
- BCM process
- Training
- Exercises
- Tests
- Management reports

Role: IT

Objective: Deliver DR for systems that is tested and maintained.

Tasks:

- Design DR solutions.
- Build/implement solutions.
- Test solutions.

Deliverables:

- Systems DR capability
- DR documentations
- DR tests

Role: Business

Objective: Identify the business's needs, prepare plans, maintain them, undertake training exercises for the staff, and participate in testing.

Tasks:

- Conduct business impact analysis (BIA).
- Conduct business continuity planning (BCP).
- Conduct education and awareness activities.
- Create call cascades.
- Plan walk-throughs.
- Perform business (WAR) and IT (DR) tests.
- Plan maintenance.

Deliverables:

- BIA
- BCP
- Info cascades
- Call cascade tests
- Plan reviews
- WAR tests
- DR tests

Role: Senior Management (Accountable)

Objective: Approve the BCM policy. Assess the capability and ensure it meets the business need and complies with the policy. Assess any gaps, risks, and issues and ensure an adequate response is in place.

Tasks:

- Approve policy and business continuity process.
- Review capability.
- Monitor issues, risks, and actions.

Deliverables:

- Approved policy
- Approved process

Role: Audit

Objective: Ensure that the business continuity program meets the needs of the business and external stakeholders.

Tasks:

- Audit policy, process, and the ongoing BCM program to ensure it meets business needs.

- Audit the BCM program to ensure that it is being efficiently and effectively executed and that it complies with the policy.

- Assess the maturity of the program against best practice and industry norms.

Deliverables:

- Audit report

Note The roles, objectives, tasks, and deliverables are generic and will depend on your organization's structure, culture, processes, and needs.

When Do You Do BCM?

The business continuity life cycle or program should keep cycling around and continually improve as it goes.

However, the steps don't have to happen sequentially. In fact, you may decide that some activities are monthly, quarterly, semi-annual, and annual, while others are ad hoc.[2] Similarly, the roles are not fixed. For example, BCM may do some of the IT responsibilities.

Business continuity doesn't just happen when there's a disaster. In fact, responding to real events is the thing that the least time is spent on. Business continuity happens day in and day out as a series of activities that prepare your organization or improve the capability to cope with events.

Standards

Standards have been devised to help organizations perform important activities in a consistent and high-quality way. They also help different organizations to work together. There are both country and international standards, and these are governed by a group of bodies that work together to promote better working practices and better working relationships.

---

[2]See Appendix C for an example timetable of events. In general, it's a good idea to make most events at least annual so that you do the business impact analysis, plan reviews, call cascade test, business (WAR) recovery test, DR tests, and so on, every year.

There are a range of standards published, and these will keep evolving over time. Probably the most widely recognized is the new International Standards Organization ISO22301, which is based on the older British Standards Institute BS25999.

Table 1-1 describes some other key standards or governance models that you may find useful.[3]

Table 1-1. Summary of BCM Standards

Standard	Comments
AS/NZ HB 221	HB 221 identifies the minimum level of acceptable performance and what infrastructure and resources are required to sustain it.
AS HB 292	HB 292 summarizes best practices from Australia, the United States, and the United Kingdom.
BCI: Good Practice Guidelines	The Business Continuity Institute (BCI) guidelines outline best practices for building or improving a business continuity program.
BS ISO/IEC 17799:2005	ISO/IEC 17799:2005 is a code of practice for information security, which includes business continuity within its scope.
BS 25777 (2008)	BS 25777 describes how to implement IT service continuity or IT disaster recovery if you prefer.
BS25999 Business Continuity Management	BS25999 provides a BCM framework and supporting management system.
DRII: Ten Professional Practices (1999)	The Ten Professional Practices established the necessary skills and competencies for individuals focused on business continuity.
FFIEC: Business Continuity Planning	The booklet outlines basic standards for BCM within U.S. financial institutions.
ISO 22301	This is the new international standard and is an evolution of BS25999, which it replaced in November 2012.
NFPA 1600	This is the established U.S. standard for business continuity. It covers business continuity, emergency management, and incident management.
TR19	TR19 is a voluntary standard that addresses the question of business continuity management and the recovery of critical processes.
SS 540	SS540 is a Singapore-based certifiable standard (that replaces TR 19 (2004)). SS540 establishes a framework for organizations to analyze and implement strategies, processes, and procedures.

---

[3]For a fuller exploration of standards, see Appendix J, where you'll find a full summary of standards.

Tip See Appendix D for a list of BCM organizations and other sources of information.

Action Plan

This chapter has introduced some basic concepts. Some may have started you thinking about your organization's current state. To help this process along, think about the following questions and what actions you should take:

1. Do you have a policy covering business continuity?

2. If you have any business continuity plans, check that they are appropriate for the key scenarios mentioned in "The Five Possible Outcome Scenarios."

3. If your organization doesn't refer to outcomes or doesn't have a continuity plan, ask yourself which are most likely to happen in your organization and which would have the biggest impact. Armed with this insight, focus on the most likely or biggest impact ones first.

4. Have you defined your requirements for business continuity in terms of recovery time and data loss (MDT, RTO, and RPO)? If not, it's time.

5. If you currently use RTO, do you need to introduce MDT? This is recommended if there is a gap between the meaning that IT and management place on the RTO.

6. Are the key business continuity objectives, tasks, and deliverables mentioned in your own company's version of "Who Does What?"

Essentials of Business Continuity Management

Kick Start Your Business Continuity

This chapter is for those with a limited (or no) business continuity plan (BCP). Its purpose is to make sure you have the bare minimum in place so you have a much better chance of surviving if disaster strikes tomorrow. Then the rest of the book will help you establish a plan that goes well beyond the minimum to enable your company to continue conducting business under duress.

BCM vs. Disaster Recovery

Many issues arise because the language we use when we talk about business continuity is ambiguous. The first thing to be clear about is what we mean when we use terms such as *business continuity* and *disaster recovery* (DR). And that clarity must extend to everyone in your organization.

Let's distinguish between business continuity and DR. Many people use these terms interchangeably. However, throughout this book, I will use *disaster recovery* to refer to the recovery of technology. Business continuity is a little more complex; it can describe the collection of related continuity disciplines: disaster recovery, crisis management, and business continuity planning. Business continuity can also describe the process of ensuring the continuity of critical operations and the supply of services or products. Finally, business continuity can also be talked about as an attribute or characteristic of an organization: "This organization has business continuity." That means it has plans in place to ensure it can survive a disaster without flinching, except in the most extreme circumstances.

■ **Note** In this book, disaster recovery will generally mean recovering the technology and systems most businesses these days rely upon. Business continuity covers DR, as well as crisis management and continuity planning.

Where Do You Stand Today? Take the Continuity Assessment

As a starting point, I strongly urge you to get a quick understanding of your current strengths and weaknesses so that you can make some informed decisions about where your immediate priorities are.

So, before you do anything else, go to Appendix E and fill in the answers. The continuity assessment is a simple tool to get an understanding of your strengths and weaknesses.

Scoring the Continuity Assessment

Each question on the assessment relates to an aspect of business continuity and is associated with at least one deliverable. For example, one of the planning elements questions is, "Does each system or IT service have a recovery plan that details the exact steps required to recover the system?" The output, or deliverable, would be a system/service recovery plan.

To complete the form, score each question between 0 and 10, with 0 being the lowest and 10 the highest.

If we take the previous example, a "10" response would be appropriate if there was a plan for every system and each plan was detailed enough to be used by a competent technician who was unfamiliar with the services. Beyond that, you are into shades of gray, especially when there is more than one aspect being considered. Don't overanalyze this; keep your response rational and simple. Broadly, this is how I rate issues: 10 equals all points covered, 7 equals the majority of points covered with limited risk, 5 equals reasonable coverage but some risk, and 3 equals little covered or increasing risk. Finally, 0 equals no coverage and significant risk.

Next decide how mature your associated deliverable or process is. The process of assessing maturity is explained fully in Chapter 10, but here's a quick scoring table:

> *0—Nonexistent:* No management processes are applied.
>
> *1—Initial:* Processes are ad hoc and disorganized.
>
> *2—Repeatable:* Processes follow a regular pattern.
>
> *3—Defined:* Processes are documented and communicated.
>
> *4—Managed:* Processes are monitored and measured.
>
> *5—Optimized:* Best practices are followed and automated.

Having done the assessment, you must next decide two things for each aspect of business continuity. First, how much do you want to implement? Second, how mature must the processes that support that aspect of business continuity be?

This is a subtle but important point. It's up to you and your management to decide how mature it needs to be. At a minimum, pretty much everything needs to be repeatable. Next review these responses, focusing on the Tier 1 questions first, then the Tier 2 questions, and finally the Tier 3s, with an eye toward prioritizing the implementation of each. (Tier 1s are the most important—the must-haves—and the 2s and 3s are of lesser importance, though still critical in many cases.) Naturally, you'll probably want to start with the Tier 1s first, then the 2s and 3s—using a little common sense and the support of your management regarding the associated priorities for your organization.

Once you know what you want to implement and how mature you want it to be, you need to finalize the priorities. It's rarely as simple as following the tiers, though they are a key factor to consider. I also think about the impact that the implementation of this or that aspect of business continuity will have on reducing risk. As I look at all the options, I also factor in how easy would it be. So, a Tier 1 that has a massive impact on the risk but is easy, cheap, and quick would be at the top of the list.

Start with the Essentials

If you are struggling at this point (and given the number of elements identified in the questionnaire, you probably are), it's worth trying to refocus at a high level on what is most important.

With this in mind, I suggest you cover the basics of business continuity, which are the following:

- Crisis management team (crisis management/crisis response)
- Call cascade (planning and testing)
- Business continuity plan (planning, education and awareness, and third-party BCM)
- DR for essential resources (capability, testing, and education and awareness)

Let's look at each in turn.

Crisis Management Team

Crisis management team sounds very grand, but in practical terms it's just the core group of people leading your organization through a crisis.

Your first order of business is to create the team. It should comprise the people who understand and can direct the critical aspects of your business.

As a rule of thumb, the key roles will probably be people from the following areas:

- *Senior management:* The crisis leader will often be the chief executive or chief operating officer.
- *HR:* This is someone who can manage any people issues.
- *Facilities:* This is someone who can manage any issues that relate to buildings and related services.
- *Communications:* This is someone who can manage the communication of information to your staff, customers, suppliers, the media, and other stakeholders.
- *IT:* This is someone who can manage any IT issues.

- *Business lines:* This is representation from the key business lines so that issues within each line of business can be managed.

- *Business continuity:* If you have a manager, this person should be on the team.

The crisis management team should be convened to tackle major issues that fall outside of what your business processes can deal with. The team's first task is to establish the facts: what, when, who, where, why, how, how many, and so on. Then they have to decide on a set of actions, some of which will be a response to what's happened. Some actions may be designed to find out more information, and some will be focused on securing additional resources.

It's important that once there is a clear issue requiring crisis management, the team comes together quickly, establishes the facts and actions, and then breaks from the meeting to execute the agreed actions. The next step is to reconvene to review actions and share updates and new information. This sequence is repeated until it is felt the issue is under control and doesn't require further crisis management.

Each person on the crisis management team is responsible for managing the flow of information from their area of the business and responding with directions and requests for more information. Where possible, they should manage the issues that emerge, track progress, and identify high-level risks and issues to the crisis leader and any other stakeholders.

See Appendix F for a detailed breakdown of tasks. These are not rigid; they provide a framework. In practice, one person may assume several roles, and other roles may be required.

WHAT MAKES A GOOD CRISIS TEAM MEMBER?

There are some behaviors and activities that are important in a crisis team member because they improve performance in a crisis. First, it's essential that they are comfortable when there is limited information and a lot of pressure to make a decision and do something. They need to able to focus on vital issues and filter trivia. They need to be good at thinking on their feet, taking in feedback, and then decisively redirecting attention based on the latest information. It's also important that they are good at providing concise updates and can keep their comments relevant to the team given the events. What is interesting to an individual, or relevant to their area, is often not relevant to the crisis management discussion.

Crisis Management Team Support

The crisis management team should be provided with some support to do the following:

- Log issues, risks, actions, and salient facts
- Track progress
- Perform any running or administrative tasks
- Set up the crisis room and facilities

Support is critical because it allows the crisis management team to focus on their responsibilities and not recording information or tracking progress. The support team helps the crisis team by presenting the salient management information in an accessible format. This may be provided by the business continuity manager, but ideally it's best if it is provided by other staff, such as executive assistants or secretaries, so the business continuity manager is free to do things such as chasing actions or communicating to key stakeholders.

Call Cascades

Perhaps the most important thing to be able to do in a crisis is quickly communicate information to staff and key stakeholders. The key issue is time. If you have to call 50 people, it will take hours to reach them all.

To speed things up, responsibility for calling people is broken down. The mechanism used is a *call cascade*, which basically sets out all the contacts and corresponding responsibility for calling people in an upside-down tree structure (Table 2-1).

Table 2-1. Simplified Example of a Call Cascade

Caller	Calls	Primary Number	Secondary Number	Other Number
Jack	Jones	0208 123 4444	01234 1234567	07456 123456
Jack	Oak	0208 123 5555	01234 2234567	07456 234567
Jack	Wood	0208 123 6666	01234 3234567	07456 345678
Jones	Ward	0208 123 7777	01234 4234567	07456 456789
Jones	Patel	0208 123 8888	01234 6234567	07456 567890
Jones	Suarez	0208 123 9999	01234 7234567	07456 678901
Oak	Keegan	0208 123 0000	01234 8234567	07456 789012

The table shows that the cascade would be initiated by Jack, who calls his three contacts, who in turn call their contacts. In this example, by the time Jack has completed his calls, Jones might have completed his too, and a few minutes later Oak has done the last call too. (See Appendix G for a more comprehensive template.)

By cascading responsibility for calling people, you have both speeded up the cascade of information and freed the person who initiates the cascade to concentrate on other activities.

The template needs to be adapted to your organization. Three cascades are probably not going to be enough. You might want to expand the concept of alternates if the primary contact is not available by adding more alternates or even giving everyone in each cascade all the contact information so that any person in the chain can complete it.

Create an Instant Basic Business Continuity Plan

Don't delay. Before you go any further, write a basic business continuity plan. Use Appendix H, simply fill in the blanks, and add the additional appendixes.

The key ingredients of the plan are as follows:

- Key contacts/roles
- How to assess the situation using the "initial response checklist"
- Escalation
- Day 0 action plan
- Call cascade
- Assembly points
- Recovery site directions
- IT plan
- Communications plan
- HR plan
- Battle box contents

The template doesn't have sections for the HR plan, IT plan, and communications plan because you have to decide whether you want to include them in the plan or have dedicated plans for each based on the template. And the battle box itself is not part of the plan.

The next few sections support the template by explaining each section of the plan.

Key Contacts and Roles

This contact list includes all the key people, third parties, emergency services, utilities contacts, conference/bridge lines, and staff emergency information numbers.

How to Assess a Situation

The initial response checklist, a simple memory aid memoir, sets out basic questions to ask when faced with a potential disaster. Using these questions will quickly enable the plan holder to decide the next steps and in particular whether to escalate or initiate business continuity plans.

Day 0 Action Plan

This is a list of the things that need to be done in chronological order. You will probably want to have several versions of the day 0 plan depending on the scenario, such as loss of IT, loss of building, denial of access to building, failure of key supplier, and so on.

Call Cascade

As mentioned, find a template in Appendix G.

Assembly Points

This section of the plan sets out where staff members should assemble if there is an evacuation of the building. You may want to have more than one marshaling point so that if a cordon is imposed around your building that includes your marshaling points, your staff will have another place to assemble.

Tip   Have alternate assembly points in the event that the first choice is inaccessible.

Directions to Recovery Sites

This part of the plan provides the addresses, contact numbers, and directions to the command center and recovery sites. Note: this may be the same location, or you may have the crisis team meeting somewhere nearer to your offices, such as in a local hotel. You may also have the IT systems being recovered into a recovery data center at one site and an alternative workspace being provided at another.

IT Plan

This may be a separate plan or a section within the BCP. It describes how to recover the specific IT services for the business. As a separate plan, it's similar to a business continuity plan but with more detail on the order of recovery. It might identify a dedicated IT recovery team that will operate in a similar fashion to the crisis management team, though the IT recovery team will be subordinate to the crisis management team.

The key is that it sets out the recovery steps. Ideally, it should record how IT would perform an orderly close down because this is often required in a disaster scenario and can often significantly minimize the impact of an outage.

Communications Plan

This part of the BCP sets out how communication with internal and external audiences will be managed. It probably includes a number of prepared messages and how communication is to be approved before being issued. It can be either a section of the BCP or a discreet plan.

HR Plan

The HR plan describes how HR issues will be managed and covers things such as accounting for staff, dealing with concerned relatives, welfare of staff and counseling for staff, expenses, travel, paying staff, HR policies, and so on. It can be either a section of the BCP or a discreet plan.

Note   Having an HR continuity strategy is essential. How will you continue to pay employees? How will you account for them in a natural disaster during work hours? What if they need counseling? You don't want to have to wing it in this area when disaster strikes.

Battle Box Contents

It's desirable to have a "battle box" ready to go at all times at the recovery sites and command center. This box should contain critical resources and documents such as work instructions, contact lists, mobile phone chargers, and so on.

This part of the plan is a list of the contents and is useful because it makes the available resources visible without having to go and physically look in the box.

Depending on the size of your organization at the affected location, you may have several battle boxes, with one for each area of the business so that people can place their own critical items in it.

Regardless of how many you may have, it's essential to keep control of them and ensure they are checked regularly and the contents updated.

In addition to a battle box, you may like to have a grab-and-go pouch. I find it useful to have some stored where I can grab them as I get evacuated. I only keep the most essential items such as the overall plan, contacts, and the like, and it could save a lot of time, especially if, God forbid, I left my phone on my desk!

The battle box list isn't essentially part of your BCP, but it's a handy place to include it.

Senior Management Involvement

Perhaps the most important ingredient to getting business continuity out of the blocks and going all the way to the line is senior management engagement.

Management involvement is key because you need their support, their resources, and probably their time and attention. They will more than likely be key sources of information, and they will have to take on some work or responsibility.

I personally like running simple exercises to get them both engaged and aware of the key issues. This also has the benefit that in instances where you have little or no plan, the outcomes from the exercise can be used as a basis for a plan.

I find it works best if you get all the senior people in a room and do a desktop exercise based on the most likely scenarios they will face. Keep it short and simple. Set out the scenario, such as the data center has burned down, and what do we do now? What will emerge is the outline of the plan as well as a clear understanding of the exposure the company is currently running without business continuity in place.

Employee Buy-in Plan

Once you have started pulling the basics of a plan together, you need to make sure that everyone involved or impacted understands their role at a time of crisis—what to do and what to expect.

Like so much of what I suggest, don't leave it to chance. Take the time to plan how you will engage your employees and raise their basic levels of awareness. The plan doesn't need to be anything grand or even formal, but it's a powerful exercise to work out what you should be doing to raise awareness, to set up the best sequence, and to give yourself some simple time-based targets.

The first thing to do is to connect to those people in your organization who regularly communicate with the staff; if you have an internal communications team or person, that's who you need. Reach out to them and take their advice about the best ways to engage the people in your organization. There's a good chance that they will be able to help you; from experience, these people are often looking for content and will happily work something into the newsletter or latest news on your intranet site.

Action Plan

Before moving on, take a few moments to reflect on the following questions and related actions:

1. Do you have a crisis management team, and is it made up of the right people? If you're not sure, review Appendix F.

2. Are all the roles that a crisis management team needs to cover included, and is the team adequately supported? If not, review "Crisis Management Team Support" in this chapter.

3. Do you have a call cascade that breaks up the responsibility for calling people in the cascade and is resilient if key people are not contactable? If not, review the template in Appendix G.

4. Do you have a basic business continuity plan, and does it cover all the basic ingredients listed in the "Basic Plan" section? If not, then review the template in Appendix H. Concentrate first on the things that will be of most use if a disaster happens now.

5. Have you taken steps to make sure that senior management is engaged? If not, then make sure either you are talking to them directly or, better still, get them together and do an exercise that gives them some experience of what they'd need to do in a crisis. It will raise awareness of any pressing issues.

6. Do you have a simple plan of action to make sure that everyone is aware of their role, what to do, and how to find out information if there is a crisis? If not, create one.

Plan for Business Continuity and Disaster Recovery

Getting Started

First Things First

In business continuity, you normally start by establishing which activities are critical in your business. You do this to ensure you'll be able to recover or protect these things if disaster strikes. The process for identifying critical activities and the resources on which they depend is called *business impact analysis* (BIA). A BIA begins with a questionnaire and answers critical questions, such as: What protections do you currently have in place? What gaps in coverage exist? How quickly can the business regain its footing? What if we lost Warehouse X to a fire, or Office Building Y to a flood, or Network System Z to a hacker?

Understand What's Critical

BIA is the process that is followed to establish what is critical to business survival and then translates this into a set of recovery priorities or requirements.

BIA comprises three activities:

1. Creating or somehow securing a structured BIA questionnaire

2. Completing the BIA questionnaire

3. Analyzing the results

Let's take a deeper look.

BIA Questionnaire

The BIA questionnaire is designed to identify what is critical and from that establish a set of requirements for business continuity. Typical requirements are a list of systems that need to be recovered and how quickly this needs to be done after an outage.

The questionnaire looks at impacts from the customer, legal, regulatory, financial, and reputational perspectives. There are also questions regarding critical resources. These resource questions establish the level of dependence on the resources and establish a recovery profile for the resource. For example, "How soon does resource X need to be recovered?" Questions help you to identify tolerances regarding the amount of data that can be lost.

Unfortunately, this sort of traditional approach is onerous, and unless you must know if each requirement is particularly driven from a regulatory, legal, financial, customer, or reputational perspective, I'd recommend a different approach.

My alternative, a more expedient BIA, can be found in Appendix I. It has a smaller set of questions and asks you to estimate the corresponding recovery time objective (RTO) in the context of a predefined material breach that can occur from the legal, financial, regulatory, customer, or reputational perspective.

Tip   Take a minute now to look at Appendix I and familiarize yourself with the BIA questionnaire. It will make the rest of the chapter much easier to understand.

However, if you prefer a longer-form BIA that requires additional question-level analysis after each BIA is completed, you can go to my web site at www.BCMDeskReference.com and download a traditional BIA template.

The top-down approach I'm advocating is quicker, because you define the criteria for a severe impact in measurable terms for your financial, legal, regulatory, customers, and reputation. Then each question is simply a test of how long it would take for an outage of a critical process, supplier, IT system, or internal dependency to lead to a severe impact. This approach takes into account all the dimensions of impact at once and delivers the ultimate requirement—the maximum time you can survive without something.

In a traditional BIA, you rate everything for each type of impact over time. This means a lot more questions then you have to reconcile the response to establish the biggest impact, in short, a lot of work.

> **Note** Either BIA questionnaire will enable you to identify critical functions, identify the resources that critical functions depend on, and quantify the impact on the business if these functions or the resources fail. It's just that the one I provide in this book is a little smarter than the other! Businesses often find that senior managers are attached to the traditional, long-form BIA questionnaire. You may just have to deal with it. If you have a choice, use the one in Appendix I. If you're like me, you do care about how you spend your time and would prefer to get a consistent and accurate set of requirements with as little effort as humanly possible. So, if you find a better approach, don't moan about mine—let me have yours!

BIA Approach

How you go about doing your BIA depends in part on the nature of your organization, in part on your strengths, and also in part on the needs of the people you're working with.

However, I'd strongly recommend doing the BIA as a facilitated session, where you ask the questions and record the responses. The alternative, handing over responsibility to the people in the business, yields less robust results.

The reason I recommend that you personally work through the BIA with department heads and other managers is in part to make their life as pain-less as possible. More importantly, you want to ensure that the responses are consistent.

For example, an equities trader in a financial firm will have a completely differ-ent attitude toward risk compared with a lawyer, and the trader's answers to the BIA will reflect this. Consequently, one person's "critical" will be another person's "medium" or even "low" impact. You need to be present to help get the most accurate answer that everyone can agree upon.

An important element of the facilitated BIA is that you give the person com-pleting it the context of the question and if necessary explain exactly what it means and what you are looking for. Another advantage is that you can test their responses by asking simple questions to determine their rationale and interpretation of the BIA questions. Testing ensures they have understood the questions and are responding consistently with the rest of the business.

Although the questions are unambiguous, there's no getting around the ambi-guity that people and their unique outlooks project on the situation.

Your approach will also probably depend on what is the best use of your time. If you have hundreds of business units to look after or a wide geographic region, you will probably be forced to rely on each unit to complete the BIA for you.

If you do decide that it's not possible to offer facilitated BIAs for all your users, then you should put in the extra work to make the BIA as clear as possible and provide some additional support materials. These might include computer-based training (CBT) and user guides.

You will also need a rigorous review process to ensure that the BIA has been completed fully and is consistent with all other BIAs.

This consistency is essential because it's the only way you can be sure you have your priorities right. To understand this, consider a situation in which you have one business unit that rates a particular process as critical and the next business unit rates the same process as merely "important." It will completely undermine any confidence you have in the final analysis.

Completing a BIA

Figure 3-1 shows the steps I recommend for completing a business impact analysis.

Figure 3-1. BIA lifecycle chart

Structure the BIA

By structuring the BIA, I mean break it down into separate questionnaires for logical parts of the business. This may not be necessary for a small business or those with a single location.

You can organize the BIA along product lines, management structure, location, facility, business lines, or whatever makes sense to your business. Ideally the structure should reflect the way the people in the business think about their business and how they tend to describe and do things.

Identify the BIA Contacts

Once you have structured the BIA, next identify who should complete each individual questionnaire and how you will approve the BIA for the unit.

The person responsible for completing a BIA is normally the manager of the area, although the manager may delegate the responsibility.

The person who approves the BIA should be the senior manager who is accountable for any failure. This person should be able to approve any investment or work required to protect the business. Approval should not be delegated below this level of accountability and power.

Schedule the BIAs

Schedule an initial BIA meeting only after you have discussed the aims of the BIA with whomever is responsible for the area. Once you have agreed on a suitable person to fill out the questionnaire, brief that person on what you're going to do and the questions you'll ask. This briefing will allow you to weigh whether you need to bring in additional people or break the BIA down into several meetings that each focus on different parts of the operation.

Once you're clear that you have found the right people, schedule the first BIA meeting.

Conduct a BIA Meeting or Interview

Try to complete the BIA in a single session. Don't rush, and, if needed, ask the person you're working with to investigate anything that is inconclusive.

You'll probably need a second meeting to finalize the BIA and—if the area is large, complex, or requires meetings with several people—you may need several more meetings.

Analyze the Responses

Analyze the responses to the BIA questionnaire and itemize your conclusions in a simple report. I cover the analysis later in this chapter.

Review the Meeting

Once you have analyzed the BIA and have a summary of the findings, meet again with the responsible manager and walk through the conclusions to make sure they match his or her understanding.

This will include any gaps that need addressing. For example, the department may be currently set up to solve problems within 24 hours, but the manager has indicated a need to complete key critical activities within 4 hours of an incident.

This review is a critical element of moderation. Believe me, when you confront people with specifics, such as when they have indicated that the payment system is needed within 4 hours but the current disaster recovery time for the payment system is 24 hours, you quickly find out what is realistic, especially if they need to spend a lot of money to achieve a 4-hour recovery!

If you have discrepancies, revisit the BIA and make the necessary changes, then repeat the review meeting until everyone is satisfied with the findings.

Approve the BIA

Once the responsible manager has confirmed the findings, arrange to meet with the approving manager. The purpose of this meeting is a further review of the BIA conclusions to get the approving manager to sign them off as a true reflection of his or her area's business continuity requirements.

This meeting can cover several BIAs, and it's normal to get sign off for both the existing risk and for any necessary remediation work.

In this meeting, you are also ratifying the issues and agreeing on actions and ownership.

Conduct a Final Analysis

Once you have completed an individual BIA and reviewed and approved the outputs, then you'll need to consolidate your findings into a single set of requirements in terms of recovery times. So, for example, you might have five BIAs that identify the same critical system, and thus you need to arrive at an overall requirement. Normally, this is the lowest requirement that gets inherited by all. So, if four areas need a system recovering within 24 hours of a disaster, but one needs it back in 4 hours, the requirement becomes 4 hours.

Finalize or Close BIA

Once the final BIA report is produced, it is management's responsibility to review the output, recommendations, and risks and then agree to a plan of action and formally accept any risks.

However, it's your job to make sure this information gets suitably presented, with actions agreed upon and ownership put in place.

Analyzing the BIA

The output of an analysis can be thought of as a consolidated statement of what is required to survive a disaster.

The result is a catalog of resources, where the relative criticality of each resource is quantified and the recovery profile is set out as a recovery time objective (RTO) and a recovery point objective (RPO). In other words, everything needed is listed with its overall RTO and RPO. Take, for example, a payment system. It might be used by 20 departments, and the recovery times could range from 5 days to 1 hour, with an acceptable data loss ranging from 1 day to nothing. Assuming that we are looking for the lowest RTO and RPO, and there are two departments that list an RTO as low as 1 hour and 10 departments have said they can't lose any data; the final analysis of the payments system will give us an RTO of 1 hour and an RPO of 0 hours.

Generally, there are two methods you can use to take the output from the BIAs and arrive at a final set of requirements:

- Weighted matrix analysis
- Threshold analysis

Let's take a deeper look at both.

Note Your goal with the final BIA is to create a document that shows what it takes to survive a disaster.

Weighted Matrix

The point of a weighted matrix is to show that not all questions are as important as others, so the logic is that they shouldn't carry the same weight when deciding on the final output of the BIA. For example, when calculating financial loss, you might decide that loss of revenue is more important than additional costs that may be incurred if an outage happened.

This is a simple methodology to adopt. First, you calculate a score for each attribute in the BIA. These attributes vary between my simple BIA and traditional BIAs. For the traditional BIA, they include impacts such as financial impact, processes impact, and systems availability. For the simpler BIA, they are things such as key activities, dependencies, outsourced services, systems, and manual workarounds.

The score is calculated by applying a weighting factor from one to five, with five being the most important, to each variable and then summing the overall score (Table 3-1).

Table 3-1. Weighted Matrix Example Based on Impacts

Financial Loss	Score	Weight	Adjusted Score
Lost revenue	5	0.4	2
Additional costs	2	0.2	0.4
Market risk	0	0.2	0
Fixed costs	0	0.2	0
Overall			2.4

This calculation is performed at a number of levels. First, you look at the individual responses to questions and attach a weighting to calculate a score for the relevant impact you are considering (e.g., financial, legal, regulatory, etc.).

For example, consider the variable "lost revenue." It contributes, on a traditional BIA, to the overall calculation of financial loss. In the BIA, the business may have indicated that the lost revenue would be "immediately" unacceptable, which for argument's sake we might score a five. If you had decided that lost revenue is most important and given it a weighting of 0.4 (out of a total of 1.0 for all elements), then the weighted score would be two.

You can weigh the various impacts to arrive at a weighted score for the business function. When repeated for all business functions, it gives a weighted score for the whole BIA. You can also apply this to resources and dependencies.

To illustrate how weighting works, consider the simplified example presented in Table 3-1.

Again, the weights when added together equal one. So to decide the weight for an individual element, look at its relevant importance against the other elements being weighed. Represent this as a fraction of one.

This example also illustrates a potential issue with weighting—that it can average out requirements. For example, lost revenue is scored at five in Table 3-1, which is the maximum. It makes sense—the levels of loss could be so massive they could take the whole business down. But this gets diluted, because it scores low on the other three elements that make up financial loss.

For this reason, I personally avoid using weighing and favor threshold analysis.

Threshold Analysis

The idea here is that you set thresholds and, if any particular impact exceeds the threshold, it establishes the requirement for a recovery time (Table 3-2).

Table 3-2. Response and Impact for Threshold Analysis

Financial Loss	Response	Impact/RTO
Lost revenue	5	2 hours
Additional costs	2	24 hours
Market risk	0	Never
Fixed costs	0	Never

In this example, we have associated an RTO with each of the possible rankings, and these are listed in a lookup table (Table 3-3). So, a response that results in a score of five, such as lost revenue, would be translated into an RTO of 2 hours.

Table 3-3. "Lookup" Table Detailing the Thresholds for Recovery Time

Lookup	
Response	RTO
5	2
4	4
3	12
2	24
1	48
0	None

The values you associate with the responses are relative to your business. So, for an investment bank, a score of five for revenue loss might reflect an order of a loss of more than $1.5 million in 2 hours. On the other hand, a retailer might adopt a loss of $100,000 in 12 hours as the criterion for a score of five response.

In practice, you'll probably want to vary the criteria for each question, so for a financial loss, a five might give you a 2-hour RTO, whereas for fixed cost, a five might only be worth 12 hours. This holds true when you look at the same question but across different businesses. For an investment bank, a five in financial loss may equate to a 2-hour RTO, but a five for the retailer might be a 12-hour RTO.

So you can see that a major task is deciding on these thresholds and how you will vary them by question relevance. In general, this will be a reflection of your business's attitude to risk and the relative materiality of the loss. For example, a $100,000 loss isn't material in an investment bank, but it could be the difference between profit and loss for a retailer.

I favor threshold analysis because it avoids the problem of averaging out high impacts and makes it easy to associate a relevant RTO with a given response to a question.

Combining Thresholds with "First Past the Post"

Combining the threshold method with an element of "first past the post" is my preferred method. However, you can also use some weighting if you prefer.

First past the post simply means that the most significant output is adopted. For example, if any impact is as low as 2 hours, then the first time one is found that is that low, 2 hours becomes the requirement.

What we do with this approach is use the lowest response time as the overall RTO. So recall that in the previous example (Table 3-2) it would be "2 hours" for overall financial loss. This makes reporting later much simpler, as you'll report on individual impacts or even functions rather than individual questions. Table 3-4 combines data for several attributes and totals them up for a final "score."

Table 3-4. Example of "First Past the Post" and Threshold Analysis

Financial Loss	Response	Impact
Lost revenue	5	2 hours
Additional costs	2	4 hours
Market risk	0	Never
Fixed costs	0	Never
Overall financial loss	5	2 hours
Legal and Regulatory	**Response**	**Impact**
Legal obligation	0	Never
Litigation likely	I	48 hours
Regulatory impact	0	Never
Overall legal and regulatory	I	48 hours
Reputation	**Response**	**Impact**
Customer impact	3	12 hours
New exposure	I	24 hours
Reputational impact	3	12 hours
Overall BIA RTO	**5**	**2 hours**

What you see here is that the lowest RTO for each section is calculated based on the first-past-the-post method (i.e., the shortest response time [impact] is carried forward and becomes the standard for the whole BIA).

Risk Analysis

In addition to knowing what the critical functions, suppliers, and systems for your business are and how quickly they must be restored in a disaster, you will want to know the most likely things that could cause a disaster.

The way you do that is by completing a risk assessment, or as it's sometimes called, a *threat assessment.*

Don't get totally distracted by threats. Take it from me—they can be very distracting as there are an infinite number of possible threats. To help manage this, I always remind people that there is a small number of ways, say four, that the threat can actually manifest itself. For example, a threat can emerge as the loss of a building, the loss of staff, the loss of the technology that you depend on, or the loss of a supplier that you depend on. Consequently, for peace of mind and to spare yourself a lot of work, you should focus on these possible outcomes based on the overall risk profile. In other words, if losing your head office building is the most likely event you will face, don't focus on all the possible things that could cause the loss of this building. Mitigate the most pressing ones and generally safeguard the building, but focus particular attention on making sure you have a plan if the building is lost, not a plan for all the possible threats.

Note You may already have a risk assessment in place and it may have identified the principle risks to your business. In general, however, performing a risk assessment beyond the BIA is outside the scope of this book.

Once you have completed a risk assessment, you need to review the risks and decide how you will handle them.

Risk assessment needs to be taken into account when you look at your recovery strategies and prioritize any investment in business continuity. If your head office and recovery site sit on the same flood plain or fault line, then you may decide that it's a good idea to review the location of your offices and consider the possibility of a secondary recovery option or moving recovery to a facility that is out of that region because the risk of losing your primary and recovery site at the same time is too high.

Risk analysis also has two other key influences on business continuity. First, it feeds into your testing, in that you should test what is most likely to happen before you test the less likely scenarios. Second, if you have issues that need fixing, you should prioritize fixing them based on risk and the ability to do the fix.

Doing a Risk Assessment

If you don't already have access to a risk assessment, you will need to refer to your organization's standard operational risk practices. Find out who is responsible for operational risk, and he or she will either be able to direct you to a completed assessment or provide you with a template.

A word of caution: it's not for you to decide what risks exist for each business area—the business has to do that. It's not even your responsibility to make sure that generic risk assessments are being done. However, you are responsible for factoring the conclusions of any risk assessment into the choice of business continuity strategy and how to prioritize any remediation work.

Risk assessment should be a regular process. If you have any policies that cover this, adhere to what they recommend; if not, I recommend that your organization schedule a full risk assessment annually and review the risk log monthly to make sure that progress is being made. When reviewing risk logs, pay particular attention to confirm that actions are progressing to plan and any mitigating measures are still effective.

Acting on a Risk Assessment

Once you have identified the key risks, you need to decide on your risk strategy—what you're going to do to manage the risks.

Basically, you have these options:

1. Mitigate the risk: Identify measures that can be undertaken that will reduce the likelihood of a risk occurring or reduce the impact it will have if it does happen.

2. Insure: In some cases you can insure against the event occurring (e.g., if stock is destroyed).

3. Transfer: In some instances you can pass the risk on to another party (e.g., you may switch to a just-in-time process so you only hold the minimum amount of inventory and hence the supplier keeps the risks).

4. Accept the risk: The accountable manager needs to formally accept the risk and acknowledge that you're doing nothing about it.

"Sanity Test" Your Risk Strategy

However you decide to mitigate your risk, you have to ask, "Would we survive if this happened?"

For example, you may insure against a threat, but if it happened and you were compensated for the direct financial loss, but lost your customers and with it your long-term revenue stream, would you survive?

Likewise, you may transfer the risk to a partner or supplier, but if they failed would you survive? There might still be some risk if their inventory gets destroyed. You don't own it. But it might mean that you can't complete your critical activities because you don't have the necessary inventory.

Residual Risk

You also need to assess what level of risk exists after you have put in place strategies for dealing with the risk.

Is this an acceptable level? If not, then you'll need to consider additional measures. For example, you may have a recovery site, but it might be located in the same district or even city, which, given the possible events, is an unacceptable risk. So you'll have to either have a secondary recovery site or change the location of the recovery site.

Action Plan

I'd recommend you look at the following actions now:

1. If you have a BIA process, does it follow the steps identified in Figure 3-1? If not, review these steps and decide if you need to change your process.

2. What methodology do you use for analyzing the BIA data: weighted matrix, threshold analysis, or perhaps something else? Regardless of your method, it should provide a consistent way of comparing the data and deciding the relative criticality. If it doesn't, then you need to rethink your methodology.

3. Has the business completed a risk assessment and is this a regular part of the business lifecycle? If not, then you need to integrate risk assessment into your processes.

Planning

Preparing the Plan

You've identified what's critical in your business, the systems you need to keep up and running, and how quickly everything must be done. Next you need a plan that brings it all together.

The business continuity plan (BCP) details what you'll need to do to keep your business running or get it back up and running in a disaster. As well as specific actions, it has all the contact details and other essential information that will get you through the first few hours.

This chapter sets out the structure of a business continuity plan and helps you write yours.

What a Business Continuity Plan Should Include

While a BCP must cover a few essentials common to all such plans, you can be pretty flexible with the order and contents. The acid test is the question "What do you need when it's 3 a.m., you have no access to your IT infrastructure, and you've just gotten a call to say the building has burned down?"

Can you pick up your BCP and in a few moments be doing the correct things?

It should be no surprise then that the organization of the content should reflect how the plan will be used. That typically means arranging the content chronologically, so the first thing you need to do is documented in the plan first.

> **Note** You know you've done a good job with your BCP when you can imagine getting a call in the middle of the night with bad news and knowing just what to do next.

Essential Ingredients of a BCP

Some content is optional and will depend on your unique business, location, situation, and so on, but I recommend you include the following topics in your plan:

- *Key contacts*: All people with a critical role in your BCP and third parties, including direct lines, conference lines, and information numbers

- *Escalation process*: Stages of an event showing how it will be detected and escalated

- *BCP checklist*: A list of things to do as soon as possible after an incident

- *Assembly point detailsBuce*: Where to go if your normal place of work is evacuated or not available

- *Priority action plan*: Critical activities to do—and who should do them—once a disaster is declared

- *Call cascade details*: Contact details for all staff covered by the plan and who is responsible for contacting whom

- *Contingency site details*: Directions to the contingency site by various modes of transport, a map, and essential supporting information such as hotels and restaurants

Other Content to Put in Your BCP

Use your judgment for your particular situation, but I suggest including the following topics in your plan (or at least your planning file):

- *Department/business overview*: Describe what you do in terms of the business process, inputs and outputs, and how you typically interact with suppliers and customers.

- *Key systems*: List your key systems, any workarounds you can employ while a system is down, and IT contact details. You might feel this is essential and belongs in the previous list, especially if you are heavily dependent on your IT.

- *Maintenance/administration*: Keep a record of changes to the plan. You might also want to describe your maintenance plan for the document—how often it will be reviewed and by whom. Cover how it will be distributed. Also, think about its relationship to other business processes. For example, you'll want to say how soon the plan will be reviewed and updated after you do a business impact analysis (BIA).

- *Testing*: Set out how the plan will be tested, such as that you will do a call cascade test yearly, a desktop walkthrough annually, a technology and end-user test annually, and so on. (I will be covering all these tests in other chapters of the book.)

- *Approval*: Keep a record of approvals required and received. Cover who, what, and when.

Before addressing the items you might include in your plan, make sure you have the essentials covered. You never know when disaster might strike, and you'll look incompetent if the only thing in your plan is "Business Overview" and "Maintenance."

Tip Cover the essentials ingredients of a BCP first, before any of the add-ons just listed. Again, it's important that the core of your plan provides the who, what, where, when, and how of getting your key processes and systems up and running again.

Structuring Your BCP

The structure of your plan may be simple, and as a result, you need only a single BCP for a location or even the whole business. However, in most organizations, the BCP is actually a hierarchy of BCPs.

You may need to have separate BCPs for each department or for each location or you may want to have business BCPs for each department and separate ones for support functions such as IT.

In fact, how you organize the plans is of little importance. What matters is that the people who need to use the BCPs are able to use them successfully and painlessly. Whatever the structure, this is your aim.

If you have multiple BCPs, it's the responsibility of the crisis management team in the event of a disaster to decide when each BCP gets invoked. They will also monitor progress and make sure that the recovery activities across different BCPs and different parts of the business are coordinated.

```
┌──────────────────────────────────────────────────┐
│                 WRITE YOUR PLAN                    │
└──────────────────────────────────────────────────┘
```

Probably the most important thing is that you get the basics down. If a disaster strikes tomorrow, you'll know you can get through it somehow.

To get you started, I've provided a basic BCP template in Appendix H. In many cases, you can just fill it in and have a workable plan. It should take only a few minutes to get the basics documented. Larger and more complex businesses will need to adapt the template or come up with something customized for their situation.

Identify What Will Trigger Your BCP

Whatever is in your BCP, it's critical that you act quickly and make sure all the people tasked with recovery actions remain coordinated.

For this to be possible, you will need a clear escalation process with clearly defined trigger points. It's not important to know the exact events that will trigger the plan. However, you will need to develop an enduring awareness in the organization of potentially disastrous events and a corresponding capability to assess the nature, impact, and need for a crisis response.

I'll have more to say on incident management and escalation in Chapter 16.

Once you have triggered an emergency response, you can direct the recovery activities virtually using conference bridge lines and similar technologies, or you may—if possible—convene as a team at a convenient location. I recommend getting together; it makes it easier to share information, and things can get missed over the phone.

When writing a BCP, keep in mind the circumstances that will force you to use it. Always keep your BCP as short as possible, easy to use, and available where it will be needed.

This last point needs expanding. Obviously, a plan is a complete waste if you can't get your hands on it when the moment of truth arrives. So, make sure you have an up-to-date copy at home, in the recovery site, and at your desk.

Tip   Keep a copy of the BCP at home just in case you get that late-night call and your office is inaccessible.

Create Battle Boxes and Grab Bags

There two items you should have accessible in case of a disaster are "battle boxes" and "grab bags."

The battle box is located at recovery locations and contains any essential equipment or resources. These can include things such as specialist stationery, hard copies of plans or directories, and any other resources that will be needed at the recovery site until you can make it back into the office.

I recommend you keep the battle boxes restricted to departmental resources and have one box per department. In addition to this, you should have generic stationery and other useful equipment stored centrally at the recovery site ready for everyone to share.

The grab bag is simply a small bag with essentials in it, such as the crisis plan and contacts list, that you can pick up on the way out—held by reception or security until it's needed—when you are forced to leave a building.

Create a One-Page Wallet Plan

I recommend creating a one-page (double-sided) summary version of your BCP. You can keep this in your wallet and have it with you at all times. You might differentiate this from the broader BCP and call it something like the *invocation, wallet,* or *page* plan.

I can tell you from experience that having a handy, easy-to-use plan has proved invaluable, especially at 4 a.m. when I've been awakened by a call and people expect me to know what to do and whom to call.

The following are key items for the wallet plan:

- BCP checklist—steps to take immediately on being notified of a potential incident
- Key contacts
- Recovery site directions
- Your cascade numbers—whom you have to call

Mitigate Risk

Your BIA will have highlighted a number of risks. You need to make sure senior management recognizes each of these and does either of the following:

- Put in place some strategies to mitigate the risk. That can be done through disaster recovery procedures, creating alternative work space, identifying alternative suppliers, or ensuring against the event happening.
- Accept the risk. That means understanding that a risk might occur and being prepared to absorb the fallout from an event.

Much of the rest of this book deals with mitigating strategies. As you deliver new strategies, you need to make sure that the BCP gets updated with some corresponding new critical activities. In other words, if you implement disaster recovery (DR) for your customer database, add some instructions to your critical activities plan to cover this.

Note   The details for IT recovery should be in a specific IT plan for that service or system, though these might be considered part of the broader business continuity planning activities.

Identify Roles

Critical to success is having clear roles associated with your BCP. These should be recorded in your key contact list.

For guidance, I suggest the following roles at a minimum:

- *Business recovery manager*: This is the person responsible for leading the recovery of your part of the business— the person executing the business continuity plan.

- *Crisis management liaison*: If your plan is one of many being centrally coordinated by a crisis management team, someone in each recovery team will need to liaise with the crisis management team. This person will report progress, issues, and risks and take instructions. This will normally involve joining crisis management team meetings or calls, providing updates, and negotiating any actions. The job is often undertaken by the business recovery manager, though be careful not to give that person too much to do.

- *Lines of business*: You will normally have representation from the different lines of business covered by the plan. They will execute their part of the plan as directed by the business recovery manager and report progress and issues to that person.

- *IT*: You may want to have an IT manager to oversee the recovery of your IT services and provide the business recovery manager with updates regarding potential business impacts, time lines for recovery, and so on.

- *Support*: I advise you have some people available to provide support activities ranging from recording events, decisions, issues, and risks on whiteboards to acting as runners to find out information or pass instruction to other teams.

- *HR*: You might want someone as part of your recovery team who is dedicated to managing staff issues such as overall welfare, remuneration, attention to injuries, and so on. It could be a dedicated HR specialist who could take on many of the responsibilities, or it may be a person tasked with liaising with the HR team and passing information to the business recovery manager. This may not be necessary if these responsibilities are covered by the crisis management team.

- *Communications*: You may also find it useful to have someone dedicated to preparing any internal or external communications. Again, this may be a liaison role with the communication being prepared and delivered centrally via the crisis management team.

- *Supplier management*: You may need someone to liaise with your suppliers.

Don't get hung up on the titles or even seeing these roles as being different people; just make sure all of the associated responsibilities are covered.

If you have the luxury of having a central crisis management team, it's normal for them to take responsibility for things such as HR, internal and external communications, security, and facilities.

Have Accountable Managers Approve Plans

I strongly recommend your BCP is reviewed by the accountable manager annually and following any major changes in the organization, systems, or facilities. This should include a formal sign-off on the latest version of the plan. I also suggest making sure you give everyone with a recovery role the latest version of the plan and ask them to review and approve it.

Action Plan

Please reflect on the following questions or suggestions and consider how you will implement any recommendations:

1. Review your BCP, taking into account the points in the section "What a Business Continuity Plan Should Include."

2. Is your business continuity plan written in a way that makes it easy to use? A good test is to imagine that it's 3 a.m. and you've just been called out of bed. Can you locate your BCP immediately and know instantly what to do next? If not, look at how it's structured, the level of detail, and so on, and decide how it can be improved so that it would pass this test.

3. Do you have a one-page plan for people to keep in their wallets?

4. Do you really need most of the things that come out of the business continuity planning process in the physical plan? Can you strip some of them out of your plan to keep things simple and doable? You can always keep important but not essential advice or procedures in electronic format.

5. Where information isn't needed in the physical plan and has been removed, can it be accessed by the people who need it in a timely fashion? For example, can the IT specialists get their detailed recovery instruction? Similarly, do the business people have access to their work instructions once they arrive at the recovery site?

6. Do you need things stored where you can grab them quickly either as you leave the office or as you arrive at the recovery center?

7. Does your business continuity plan set out clear roles? If not, you should identify who will be leading the recovery activity and who will be available to undertake the recovery steps.

8. Does someone review and approve the plan contents, and if so, are they the right people?

IT Disaster Recovery

An Overview of IT Disaster Recovery

IT disaster recovery, or DR for short, is the side of business continuity that deals with protecting and recovering your critical IT services. This chapter explains the basic concepts of DR and tells you what you'll need to do to set it up and keep it running. Besides basic strategies for keeping your IT up and running, I provide basic definitions of the concepts all managers involved with business continuity should understand, along with tips on identifying risks and creating a DR plan that has the approval of top managers.

What Is DR?

IT DR refers to both the way that systems are protected from a disaster and the process that is followed to recover them in a disaster.

DR predates business continuity and was something that IT people started to think about quite soon after computers started being used for commercial applications. What they realized, as organizations became ever more dependent on their systems, was that they needed a way to get the business back up and running if the computer went down.

The main scenario they identified was the computer network failing and not recoverable at the site that it normally runs from.

In practical terms, it's almost always preferable to recover the production system in situ rather than switching operations to a DR machine, which might be located hundreds or even thousands of miles away. However, you have to face the real possibility that the primary site is not available.

Risks and Issues Associated with DR

There are often risks and issues associated with running information systems in DR mode. The biggest risk is that for some unforeseen reason your DR solution won't work. In addition, there's the risk associated with switching physical systems between the production environment and the DR environment. You could lose data or corrupt it.

You also need to weigh the level of service that you will receive when you attempt to deliver your production services from the disaster recovery system. It's quite common for the DR system to have a smaller capacity machine that has been sized to run just essential work.

Finally, there are the risks associated with the switch back to production, or "normal operations" as I will call it. These are similar to those associated with invoking DR: loss of data, data corruption, service outages, and in the worst case a complete failure to be able to resume "normal operations" from your regular production environment.

DR Solutions for IT

There's a wide range of DR solutions. These solutions are driven by business requirements such as recovery time objective (RTO) and recovery point objective (RPO) and by constraints such as budget and location and how much you are willing or able to afford.

Broadly speaking, solutions can be broken down into the following categories:

- Hot standby
- Warm recovery
- Cold recovery
- Resilience
- Mobile recovery

Let's look at each one in more depth; note that later in the chapter I define some terms that might be familiar to IT professionals but perhaps not to managers in other areas.

Hot Standby

As the name suggests, this is ready-to-go DR. Basically you have the production environment reproduced at your DR site in a constant state of readiness. The hardware is adequately sized to run production work, the operating system is up and running, the data is an exact copy (within a second) of production, and the applications are ready to take over production work.

Hot Standby Architectures

Providing such a high level of service requires the following:

- Replicated data
- Replicated hardware
- Replicated software
- Running in ready state
- Normally in-house
- Live/passive
- Mirrored data
- Rapid/automated failover

Hot Standby Capability

Recovery time varies from a few seconds, if you adopt a fully automated solution, to a few hours if you have to include management sanction and manual intervention. This is often more a matter of your organizational culture than the technology. Data loss is normally down to 1 second or less.

Hot Standby Costs and Complexity

Hot standby is complex and may have geographic constraints. For example, data centers may need to be within 15 miles (25 kilometers) of each other if you need to support synchronous data replication. This is applicable to architectures where the data must be written to both sites, and the writes must be confirmed before the next transaction can be performed.

This architectural constraint is normally linked to the specific application that will have to be written as a synchronous application. Note that this is not a trivial application constraint that can be changed easily!

By contrast, with asynchronous applications you write the data to the DR computer but don't wait for confirmation before continuing. This type of DR capability lends itself to separation over larger distances. Such systems are called *geographically dispersed*.

Costs for hot standby are high because it requires a dedicated solution that is maintained as part of the production environment.

Hot Standby Benefits

Hot standby has many benefits, including the following:

- Almost no loss of data

- Nonstop potential for your operations to continue production work when essential maintenance is being undertaken on the production environment

- Reduced manual intervention, which means reduced risk

- High reliability

- Low risk of failure during invocation because you are dealing with a known architecture and a limited number of steps to recover it

Warm Recovery

Warm recovery is similar to hot standby in that the hardware is configured ready to run the main production workload. In other words, the operating system and applications are maintained in a state of readiness on the DR machine.

By ready, I mean maintained and up to date, but offline and without all the latest application data loaded. Warm recovery systems are generally offline and need to be rebooted, and all the applications need to be started from scratch. In general, the data also needs some manual intervention before production work can begin, which further adds to the delays and risk.

It's normal practice to maximize the use of warm recovery hardware. For example, when hardware is not being used for production work as part of DR, it is used to run noncritical work such as development, testing, and so on. This maximizes the use of expensive hardware. However, it adds to recovery time because the noncritical workload needs to be closed down and the DR environment brought up.

Obviously, warm recovery solutions must be adequate to run the projected volumes in DR mode. Bear in mind, though, that in DR the volumes may be considerably less than you'd normally run. In some cases, however, they can be higher because you may have to cope with a large amount of pent-up demand that has been building during the outage.

Typical warm recovery characteristics include the following:

- Replicated hardware, generally offline and used for noncritical workload.

- Software built ready to go. This should be change controlled as part of the production environment. Normally, the software is not running between events.

- Mirrored data, data vault, or tape-based data (perhaps virtual).

Warm recovery solutions are often provided by specialist third parties. This is cheaper but reduces the level of control or your ability to test.

Warm Recovery Capabilities

Typical RTOs for warm recovery are normally greater than 4 hours and typically 8–12 hours. This depends principally on the data and how it's restored. If you need to restore data from tapes, this process can take days.

It's critical that you know exactly how much data you have and how long this would take to load in a recovery scenario. Testing systems in isolation may not be an accurate guide because you have to factor in the impact of potentially having to recover many applications in parallel, which will lead to conflicts and contention between applications all trying to use the same hardware, networks, and people.

Data loss, or the recovery point objective, depends on the specific architecture. If mirroring is used, it can be as low as a second. This depends on how the mirroring is configured. If restoration is tape based, the RPO depends on the frequency of backups and when the data was taken off-site.

Warm Recovery Cost and Complexity

The architecture for warm recovery is less complex than hot recovery or resilient solutions, but it can often be more complex to invoke because it requires more manual intervention and consequently presents more potential areas that can fail.

Overall, no DR is cheap, but warm recovery is significantly cheaper than hot standby. You simply need to balance the costs against the risks.

Warm Recovery Risks

Because of the level of manual intervention required and the need to coordinate recovery actions across a number of different IT and business disciplines, the risk of either failing to recover or experiencing delays is medium to high.

There are also significant risks of data loss when data recovery is dependent on tapes. The key risks are that backup tapes remain on-site and therefore not available. Another risk is that one of the tapes is unreadable, rendering the whole set unreadable and forcing you to recover from an earlier set.

Regular testing and training are critical to the viability of warm solutions. Also important is the backup strategy adopted and consequently how an overall recovery is affected if a single tape is unreadable.

Tip Ask yourself, "What would be the outcome if this backup tape failed when DR has been invoked?" If tape failure is unacceptable in any scenario, you'll need to invest in a more robust solution.

Warm Recovery Benefits

Warm recovery benefits include the following:

- Lower costs
- More likely to work than cold recovery
- Quicker than cold recovery
- Third-party services are possible, possibly removing the need for a DR site

Cold Recovery

Unlike hot recovery and warm recovery strategies, cold recovery doesn't have any hardware or software prepared or ready to run.

Generally, the hardware is allocated. In other words, it is on the floor in the data center and has required power and network connectivity. However, the hardware needs to be configured. The operating systems and applications are often built but are probably not loaded. Last but not least, the application data will also require loading onto the cold recovery configuration's storage.

Overall, cold recovery requires a lot of manual work. From experience, I can tell you that you may find that the actual configuration that is used on the day you need it is not the same as was last tested. So, you need to be mindful that the configuration you end up working with is to a degree untested. Consequently, you should expect unanticipated delays.

Cold recovery is often provided by third-party specialist companies, and as such it reduces the cost and need to maintain an extra data center. However, you lose flexibility and control over when you can test and, in particular, retest. You also miss out on the opportunity to leverage your DR environment for other uses, such as testing and development.

Cold Recovery Architecture

The architecture for a cold recovery configuration is simple, especially if a third-party solution is required. In general, the DR configuration should be adequate to run the projected volumes of work in a DR situation. Remember that in DR the volumes may be considerably less than you'd normally run. However, they can be higher because you may have to cope with a large amount of pent-up demand that has built up during the outage.

The cold recovery system must also be able to run the latest production operating system and applications. There are plenty of examples of where people have invoked their DR plan only to find that the hardware is no longer able to run the production system, which has been upgraded since the last test.

If you're using third-party solutions, keep in mind they are normally provided using a pool of available hardware and consequently will vary on the day based on what's available.

Third-party DR suppliers make their money by selling the use of their equipment to multiple parties, and it's your responsibility to make sure that your software will run on the available configuration. Don't think for a minute that because you've outsourced the delivery you have outsourced the responsibility to make sure it works!

Tape or data vault requires lengthy data recovery, and there is a high level of manual intervention required to recover cold solutions.

Note   Just because you have outsourced a recovery solution to a third party doesn't mean you have outsourced the responsibility you have to ensure it works the way you want it.

Cold Recovery Capability

The recovery time depends on how the data is recovered and how much of it there is. However, if you are using a third party or run noncritical work on the hardware during normal operations, there will be a period of up to four hours to clear down the environment. In the case of third-party solutions, they will make this a specific time on the contract. For example, it may say you will not be allowed access to the facility or environment for at least four hours.

Data loss, or the recovery point objective (RPO), depends on the specific architecture. If data vaulting or mirroring is used, the RPO can be as low as a second. This depends on how the mirroring is configured. However, if a tape-based architecture is used, then it depends on the frequency of backups and how quickly the tapes are taken off-site.

Cold Recovery Cost and Complexity

The architecture for cold recovery is the least complex, but it is more complex to invoke because of more manual intervention, significant logistical challenges such as moving tapes, and getting access to third-party locations. Consequently, there more potential points at which you can fail.

Overall, no DR solution is cheap, but this is significantly cheaper than hot or warm standby. If your organization owns its own cold recovery DR hardware, rather than using a third-party DR service, you can use it to run noncritical work such as development, testing, and nonessential business applications. This can further reduce costs and help with the business case.

Cold Recovery Risks

Because of the high level of manual intervention and the need to coordinate recovery actions across a number of IT teams, business departments, and third parties, the risk of failure to recover or experience delays is high.

As with warm recovery, there are also risks of data loss if you depend on tape. If you do, make sure backups exist off-site and test to ensure they work as you expect them to work. If a tape is unreadable, you will have to recover from an earlier set.

Regular testing and training are critical to the viability of cold solutions. However, where third parties are used, this is often difficult. For example, you may get only one guaranteed test slot per year, and additional test slots (if available) come at a high cost.

Complexity and Cost of Cold Recovery

Cold recovery means a simple architecture. However, it will require significant levels of manual intervention and is consequently prone to issues because each invocation often utilizes a unique configuration.

Again, you have to bear in mind that if you are putting the hardware to non-DR uses, it will take time to close down. Also, you have to assess how long you can go without whatever it is that is being replaced by DR.

Cold Recovery Benefits

Cold recovery has a number of benefits, including the following:

- Lowest costs

- Using a third party can remove the need for a dedicated DR site and associated costs

- If dedicated hardware is used, then you can reduce the overall costs further by running a noncritical workload when in standby in case of a disaster

Resilience

Resilience isn't a disaster recovery strategy. Rather, it is a way of avoiding the need for DR in a number of scenarios. Specifically, it can avoid the impact of localized component failures. For example, if the resilient solution is to split services between two data center halls each with independent power, air conditioning, and network connectivity, you can avoid a loss of service in the event that a single data center is lost.

However, a solution like this doesn't necessarily remove the need for DR.

Often, resilience is provided within the same data center, and as such, the solution is exposed to the consequences of localized failures such as loss of power, cooling, communications, buildings, people, or shared infrastructure.

However, given a lower likelihood of a failure, you may decide to spend less on your DR solution. For example, you might adopt a warm recovery capability rather than hot standby if you have a highly resilient production machine on the basis that the risk of needing to invoke is much lower.

To make this decision, you need to be led by the facts and in particular know how long you can survive without the service. If you need to have a service back quicker than is possible with warm recovery, it becomes something of a no-brainer to move to hot standby.

Resilient architectures can be thought of as one of a number of possibilities:

- Nonstop fault tolerant

- Live/live, geographically dispersed

- Live/live, locally dispersed

- Live/passive, geographically dispersed
- Live/passive, locally dispersed

I will discuss each in turn in the coming pages.

Resiliency Risks

Though resiliency solutions reduce the likelihood of an outage, it doesn't eliminate the possibility. You can still lose power, communications, and other things that will affect the whole system. For this reason, resilience is, as we just discussed, generally used in combination with DR. Though, given the overall benefits of resilience, you may decide to spend less on DR and have a slower DR strategy.

Resilience Costs and Complexity

Recent years have seen the costs of resilience reducing rapidly as the underlying costs of components have become commoditized. This is being accelerated as operating systems and applications provide increased support for resilience. As a simple rule of thumb, you should probably multiply the build/implementation costs by a factor of three over a nonresilient architecture. However, the run costs are probably slightly greater than double.

In many instances, the benefits are so significant from a purely operational point of view that the cost case stands up without factoring in business continuity.

Benefits of a Resilient Architecture

The benefits of increased resiliency include the following:

- Increased system availability
- No downtime for component maintenance
- No outages when components fail

Table 5-1 sums up the differences of the approaches just discussed.

Table 5-1. Comparison Between Recovery Strategies

Type	Cost/Complexity	Recovery Time	Data Loss
Cold recovery	Low/simple	24 hours	Last backup
Warm recovery	Medium/moderate	4–24 hours	Last backup/mirror
Hot recovery	High/complex	0–4 hours	Seconds
Resilience	Very high/very complex	0	0

Mobile Recovery

Mobile recovery covers a range of solutions. Instead of relying on a traditional data center to host your recovered site, you use a temporary solution that is moved to your desired location.

These come in a variety of shapes and sizes ranging from trailers that are towed to your site to extensive mobile data centers that are built on-site.

They require that you have adequate space to park the mobile recovery facility and, ideally, access to network and utilities.

Mobile recovery is an option offered by most DR solutions providers. I'm not aware of anyone who has their own in-house mobile solution.

Like shared DR, these solutions are syndicated between a number of clients so aren't normally configured ready to go. The trailer-based solutions are normally configured at the time of invocation but before leaving the depot.

Mobile Recovery Risks

Many risks are associated with this sort of a strategy, and many will be unique to your deployment.

However, the key risks are as follows:

- A solution is invoked by another client when you want to use it. (This is a significant risk if, say, a number of businesses are affected by the same flood.)

- The supplier is unable to get the mobile recovery solution to your site, perhaps because of the event that is causing your outage.

- There's a technology failure and delays are longer than traditional DR because required components or specialists are not available at the recovery location.

- The planned location for your mobile recovery is not available at the time of recovery.

Basic DR Concepts and Technology

Let's take a step back and look at some of the basic concepts all IT people and business recovery managers should know when it comes to IT disaster recovery.

Mirroring

Mirroring is a disk-based technology that creates a mirror (identical) copy of your production data on a secondary disk system. The mirrored disks can be at a remote data center.

Asynchronous mirroring means that the mirror is written independently of the main disks. In other words, the application doesn't have to wait until both the main and mirror disks are updated before it does the next thing.

Synchronous mirroring means that the application that is updating the disk has to wait for the mirror as well as the main disk to confirm that the update was successful before it can continue. This wait time can become an issue as distance between the main disk and mirror increases the time it takes to transfer the data. The increased time delay can seriously undermine performance and in many cases can cause the system to time out.

Consistency Groups

An issue with recovering distributed systems is that application or services data may be backed up to a different point in time. As a result, when you recover everything, or even a single failed component, you can have discrepancies between the services backups that make up the whole system.

Consistency groups provide a useful solution for this by ensuring all the relevant services data is recovered to the same point in time so that you will never have a situation where, say, a transaction was reflected in one part of a distributed system but not in another. For example, if a transaction is visible on the ledger but not on the order book, this leads to problems of reconciliation and puts the data integrity of the whole system into doubt. When you implement a consistency group, you know all the data is recovered to the same point in time.

Tape-Based Recovery

Used for decades, physical tapes store data and are used, if needed, to restore it. With modern disk systems, physical tapes are not normally the primary mechanism these days for ensuring data recovery or integrity, but if there are data integrity issues or the failure is catastrophic, they are a useful secondary resource.

There are different strategies for backing up data, and these strategies are important to understand when it comes to tape. There can be significant repercussions in terms of backup duration and the potential for losing data.

The keys to tape backup and consequently your ability to recover are frequency and backup strategy employed. For example, how long do you go between backups? Do you use differential or incremental backup? What's your policy on removing tapes from the site? All are key factors.

Backup frequency is something you need to give serious thought to. The key question is, how much data can you afford to lose? If it's one day's worth, you can afford to have just one daily backup, and so forth.

Backup strategy is a balance between operational efficiency when taking backups and the integrity of data when you recover. Your choice here is differential or incremental backups.

Differential backups record all the changes since the last full backup each time a backup is run. This means that to recover fully, you need only the last set of tapes from the last full backup and the tapes from the last differential backup. The downside is that you need to use more tapes and more time each time you run a backup.

Incremental backups save only the changes since the last incremental. This is a much quicker backup to run because it saves far less data and writes less tape. However, to restore the data, you need the last full backup set and every incremental backup tape, too. If any incremental tapes are unreadable, the whole restoration is at risk.

The strategy for removing backup tapes off-site is critical so that the tapes are both quickly accessible and not still in the building when something goes wrong.

Tip   Create a firm policy for removing backup tapes and identifying who will do so, when, and where the tapes will end up. If the worst happens and your backup tapes go up in flames, your troubles have only just begun.

Virtual Tape

This is a disk system that acts and is accessed just like a tape system. It has a number of advantages over tape, including speed, physical storage space (no need for extensive rack space in physical libraries), no wasted tapes, and no mechanical delays while tapes are found, loaded, and read.

Virtual tape also makes it possible to create, update, and delete virtual tapes that are at a secondary location if, say, your backups are off-site and therefore secure at the point of creation.

Tape-only solutions are becoming less common, and virtual tape is replacing many enterprise backup solutions. However, virtual tape still relies on physical tape as the ultimate backup medium. That's because virtual tape is itself only a backup to tape.

Cross-Site Tape

This is where the physical tape system is at a remote location. For example, your backups are off-site and therefore secure at the point of creation. It can be used in combination with virtual tape so that you are in fact writing to a virtual tape device at the remote site.

Backups

There are three basic strategies for backing up: full, incremental, and differential.

Full Backup

Full backup is where all the data, not just the things that have changed since the last backup, gets saved. It can be quite a long process and sometimes difficult to complete in the available time. Recovering all the data is simpler, however, because you just need to read the full backup.

Incremental Backups

Incremental backup describes a process where you save only the things that have changed since the last backup. This is much quicker. However, restoring all the data requires that the last full backup is read, and then all the incremental backups have to be read to restore all the data to its latest state. If any backups are missing, the whole process can fail, and you have to revert to the last complete set of data.

Differential Backups

Differential backup is where every change that has been made since the last full save is saved. This takes longer than an incremental but has the advantage that when it comes time to restore the data, you need to read only the last differential plus the last full backup.

Live/Live

Live/live refers to an architecture where the processing is split between two physical machines that are independent in the sense that one machine can continue to work without the other. Live/live architectures vary; in some instances, the actual work is done on both in parallel or is routed to whichever part of the whole architecture is most convenient.

Checkpoints

A *checkpoint* is a system process that allows you to capture the current state of an application so that it can be recovered to the checkpoint if required. It's not useful in a DR situation but could be useful for restoring localized problems.

Transaction Logs

Transaction logs are files that record all the transactions that have taken place and can be stored off-site. They are used to reprocess all the work that has been completed since the last backup. If the transaction logs are available at the DR site, they can be used to recover a given application back to the last recorded transaction, not just the last backup. In other words, the application can be recovered to within seconds of a disaster, not the start of day. If disk mirroring is employed, then the value of transaction logs is greatly reduced.

Nonstop Fault Tolerant

This architecture emerged as a commercial proposition in the early 1980s as a solution for running high availability services like ATMs in banking. The basic idea is that every component in the system is duplicated such that if a component fails, the system continues running by instantly switching to the backup component.

Increasingly, this is a standard architectural feature where within each component there is resilience built in and the whole system is designed with redundancy built in.

Geographically Dispersed Live/Live

This means that the system is configured such that it extends across two or more sites that are geographically removed from each other. However, unlike hot recovery and live/passive, both sites undertake production work. Ideally, all sites should have independent power, water, and communications and not share the same threats—such as they are both in a city center location prone to flooding.

It's normal for a geographically dispersed system to be located at two sites, and I've worked on that assumption in this section. But it is possible to have more than two sites or "nodes," as they are sometimes known.

The configuration needs to be sized such that either site can take on a full workload. Normally, the workload is split between either site, and data is recorded at both. Figure 5-1 provides a visual description.

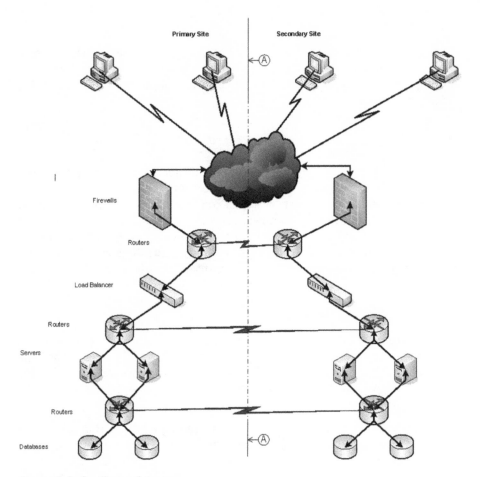

Figure 5-1. Resilient architecture

As Figure 5-1 shows, work can be executed at either site, depending on available resources. So if the primary site is busy, it will be done at the secondary site. When records are changed, created, or deleted, the action takes place on both sites. However, exactly how this is done may vary; both disks might be written to at the same time, or the local disk might be written to first and then the second site soon after.

Normally any failover—switching from one computer to another if there's a problem—will be invisible to the end users because the workload simply gets routed to the available node.

The system should be configured so that a single node has enough capacity to support peak volumes, and the users shouldn't even experience significant performance degradation.

Bringing the failed node back online should also be transparent to the users.

Locally Dispersed Live/Live

This is similar to geographically dispersed live/live except that the solution resides in a single data center. It looks exactly like the diagram of the geographically dispersed service in Figure 5-1 except the nodes are in the same location.

Sometimes each node will reside in a different data hall. If possible, they should have independent power, cooling, and communications, so if you lose supply from one source, the other node will continue running using its independent supply.

Geographically Dispersed Live/Passive

This is similar to the geographically dispersed live/live, but live work is not processed on both legs. The primary node is live and does all the work; the other is in a state of readiness to take over if the live leg fails. It's like hot standby except there's not a separate DR machine. It's all part of the same machine, under the control of the same operating system.

Data is processed on the live node and recorded to both sites. There may be some lag between the live and passive nodes, and it is possible to lose the odd transaction. Failover is normally automated and occurs with almost no impact on the users, who will probably be totally unaware. Both legs should have exactly the same capacity and configurations.

Locally Dispersed Live/Passive

This is similar to the geographically dispersed live/passive, but both nodes are hosted in the same dame data center. Ideally, like its geographically dispersed equivalent, each node will reside in a different data hall within the data center. If possible, each node should have independent power, cooling, and communications; so if you lost supply from one source, the other source would continue running.

DR Roles and Responsibilities

Roles and responsibilities in a DR situation change from organization to organization depending on many local factors including structure, size, and industry. The following is not definitive but sets out the high-level responsibilities and roles.

Table 5-2 is a CAIRO matrix that maps responsibilities (including oversight) against roles and defines if the role is/has

C = Consulted so that their requirements and feedback is included

A = Accountable for making sure it's done and meets business needs

I = Informed about what has happened

R = Responsible for doing a job

O = Oversight of the deliverable, process, or activity

Table 5-2. DR Roles and Responsibilities: CAIRO Matrix

Responsibility	Business Continuity Manager	Business Process Owner	IT	Management
Define a DR policy.	CO	CI	R	A
Identify business recovery requirements for each system.	R	C	C	AIO
Assess current capability and identify gaps.	R	I	C	AO
Agree on remediation and/or new DR requirements.	C	C	R	A
Develop DR solutions to meet new requirements or address gaps.	IO	C	R	A
Test DR solutions.	CIO	CI	R	AI
Prepare a data center recovery plan.	CIO	C	R	A
Prepare individual DR plans.	CIO	C	R	A
Maintain plans.	CIO	C	R	A
Initiate recovery.	R	I	C	A
Clear down environment.	I	I	R	CA
Organize logistics at the recovery site (rooms, food, travel, etc.).	I	C	R	A
Determine recovery order based on previously agreed criticalities (data center recovery plan) and current business priorities (what's relevant—such as it might be end of year, making finance more critical than normal),	C	C	R	AC
Perform individual recovery actions (i.e., make systems available).	I	I	R	A
Perform acceptance testing.	C	RA	C	I
Bring systems online.	I	CI	RA	I
Revert from DR to production.	CI	CI	R	AO

DR and Projects

It's probable that when you understand business requirements in terms of systems recovery and then compare this to what is currently possible, there will be gaps. In a quarter of a century of working for some of the biggest and most risk-averse organizations, I've never worked anywhere that didn't have gaps! To address this, the gap needs to be formalized. Document it as a risk, produce a business case, and initiate a DR project to fix the gaps.

In addition to what I call DR projects, you have normal business change. Now if you're ever going to close the gaps, you need to prevent, as much as possible, new gaps from emerging. The key to this is to embed DR and business continuity into all of your change projects so that emerging or changing requirements are delivered when it's easiest and most economical to do so. You want them to be part of the project that's changing your business in the first place.

The thing you can't do is stop the world from changing, so in this sense it is both healthy and normal for the requirements to change over time.

Documenting DR Risks

I'm not going to go too deep here with documenting risks because most companies already have a framework, templates, and processes to follow.

I will suggest two things that will help you get traction as you try to initiate a DR project to address any gaps between risks and your ability to mitigate them.

- Try to document the risk and not the threat. Don't just document, for example, that payments don't have a DR plan. Think of the consequence of that, so the consequence or risk is that "systemic failure for the U.S. financial system."

- Make sure you have identified the person who is accountable, and make sure they are in fact held accountable for the risk. This person must be empowered to address the issue or sign off on the risk.

In effect, what I'm saying is highlight the risk, try to attach it to something that is already visible and a cause of focus, and then make sure that those who can do something about it are aware and compelled to include fixing the gap in their priorities.

Preparing a DR Business Case

Consider the following when you prepare the business case for addressing a gap.

Consult your finance department and get direction on exactly what makes a winning business case. You really don't want to keep going backward and forward—get it right first time.

Identify any mandatory requirements and make them the focus. For payments in Hong Kong, for example, you may have to demonstrate recovery within two hours for your payments system as a prerequisite for membership of the CHIPS payment system.

Decide what would be an acceptable level of residual risk. In other words, identify the acceptable level of risk that remains after the project is completed. Ensure that you understand the residual risk and make sure this is consistent with the risk appetite of your organization.

Assess a range of solutions and select the one that matches the risk appetite. Identify the ongoing, running costs of the solution and factor them in.

Don't wait until you finally and formally submit the business case for it to see the light of day. Make sure that all the key people who will be deciding on it are aware of what's in the business case and that they have bought into it. Decision day is not the day to be educating people on the finer points of your business case. So, the message is get out there, speak to people, and take their input on board; then go back to them until you can get them to say "yes."

Make the decision a "no-brainer" for the person you must persuade. Don't just rest on your laurels. Do a thorough job and speak to finance, getting guidance so you can present your case in the desired format. Last but not least, engage all the stakeholders to gather their input and secure their support before the case gets submitted for approval.

Undertake a DR Project

Delivering the required DR capability, whether that's starting from the ground up, enhancing an existing solution, or engaging a third party, can be considered a project because it has the following:

- Defined goal
- Starting point
- Deliverables
- End point

Also, regardless of what type of project it is, it will have the following steps:

1. Set out the requirements
2. Evaluate the possible solutions
3. Select the solution
4. Detail the design
5. Build
6. Test
7. Implement
8. Sign off/close down

The business case should align with these steps, but exactly how you go about the project will be driven by your organization's process.

You might not be the project manager, so the key for you is to ask questions and make sure the basics are being done.

The following list is a good starter:

Make sure the project is formalized. It needs to be documented, with an agreed schedule of work, allocated resources, identified risks and issues, regular progress reports, clear ownership of the project, and responsibility for managing the work.

Make sure the solution will meet your business requirement. If it has to be recovered in four hours, for example, how will this be achieved, and what reasons do you have to believe this?

Make sure you understand the solution that is being proposed. If you don't understand what's being proposed, something is seriously wrong because this is fundamentally simple stuff. The fault here is not with you but with whoever is explaining it to you.

Keep asking the simple questions: what, when, why, how, where, and who. Keep at it, and don't ever feel stupid for asking questions or allow yourself to be intimidated. If you ask and still don't get it, ask again and again and again.

Ask, if people bombard you with noise and technobabble, "So what?" You will be surprised how after a few iterations of "Yes, but so what?" you can quickly discover that you're about to pay for a platinum-plated white elephant, when you just need a no-frills solution.

Make it your responsibility to sign off the deliverables against the detailed design and functional requirements so you can be sure that your requirements are being met.

Make sure people know at the outset that you're going to need to sign off.

Understand why the final solution was chosen, why the others were rejected, and what compromises have been made. Think. Will all the requirements be met? Has the accountable person been made aware and agreed?

The Change Process

It's highly likely that you will need to improve the culture or process for change within your organization. You can't afford to engage in every change to make sure that contingency and resilience requirements are included and accurate.

What you need to do is embed business continuity and DR into the change process. In particular, you need to make sure that all project managers do this without having to remember to do it. If people have to remember business continuity and DR, then all is lost.

In other words, you need to include business continuity and DR in things like the following:

- *The project process:* This makes business change management (BCM) part of every project and something the project managers are responsible for.

- *Project templates:* Help people by prompting them as they do their projects.

- *Project checklists:* Again, this is an excellent way to remind people to include business continuity and disaster recovery.

- *Business objectives:* Make people in the business accountable for their business continuity and set out some standard business objectives.

- *Project sign-off:* This should be at every stage of the project and not just the end. Make it mandatory. If DR isn't tested and documented, the system can't go live.

Get DR Going Live

Making sure DR works shouldn't be an issue at this point. With adequate testing, that should be a given.

Rather, the following items are key:

- Making sure the DR system is documented.

- Making sure that if any business continuity plans are affected, they have been updated to reflect the changes.

- Making sure that support responsibility for the service, and DR in particular, is defined and agreed on.

- Making sure that there is adequate funding to cover ongoing testing and maintenance.

- Making sure that your new DR solution is tied to the production environment it covers. That means if production changes, DR must be changed and tested too.

- All these points should be covered by the policies that cover DR.

Action Plan

Please review these questions and consider how you should respond to any recommendations:

1. Have you identified a clear set of business requirements that list which systems you need recovered, how quickly (RTO), and the amount of data loss that would be acceptable (RPO)? If you have solid requirements, have the business owners signed off on them?

2. If you have any existing DR solutions, are they able to meet business requirements in terms of recovery time (RTO) and data loss (RPO)? If not, then you need to revisit your business impact analysis process.

3. Is DR tested and done regularly enough? If not, then review Chapter 8.

4. Are the tests meaningful? Do they prove that the DR will actually work?

5. Are the right people involved in business continuity? Is it owned, and are there appropriate policies and controls? If not, then review the section "DR Roles and Responsibilities."

6. Are any issues or risks documented? Are the people accountable for the exposure aware and responding appropriately?

7. Is there adequate funding for business continuity, or do you need to create a new business case? If not, then review the section "Preparing a DR Business Case."

8. Is business continuity an integral element of your change process? If not then, review the section "The Change Process."

9. Are there strong controls that prevent systems from going live without proven DR? If not, then review the change and release processes.

Business Recovery Strategies

Identify Your Approach

Business recovery is all about how to keep your critical business processes going. This chapter explains the key aspects of business recovery and how you can get procedures and policies in place as quickly as possible.

What Does Business Recovery Involve?

At times of disaster, any function will have some sort of business continuity requirement. These requirements range from continuing the function regardless to suspending the function until the business recovers. Keep in mind that doing nothing is a decision; you either decide to do something or time slips through your fingers and the decision to do nothing is made for you. So if your plan is to do nothing, make sure it's a conscious decision.

To achieve your desired recovery requirements, you will have to decide on a range of strategies that will enable you to achieve the desired state. They can be simple, such as setting up simple processes and arrangements, or they can be complex, such as building duplicate facilities to which you can shift operations at the time of crisis.

Some of the strategies are achieved by simply documenting them and referencing them in the relevant plans. Others will require extensive funding and significant projects to deliver and maintain them.

Regardless of their complexity, your business continuity plans must be changed to set out how and when the strategies will be deployed.

Understand Resilient Functions

Functions or activities that must continue uninterrupted are not dealt with by business recovery. Or more precisely, resilience is not the same as business recovery. If you need resilience—the ability to bounce back quickly if not immediately from disasters—then this needs to be built into your systems, locations, supply chain, people, and so on.

Resilience typically applies to ultra-critical tasks and is often associated with high-risk, zero-tolerance-for-downtime industries such as air traffic control, nuclear power generation, and so on.

Of course, this all goes back to your business impact analysis (BIA), where you distinguish those things that need resilience from those that can tolerate some downtime.

Note Understand the difference between recovery and resilience. In most cases, your job is to recover business functions over time (even if that time is short). Resilience, however, is all about doing the best you can to keep functions up and running no matter what is going on. As a result, it requires much more planning and much more money to deliver.

Understand Recoverable Functions

The majority of activities and functions can tolerate a degree of disruption, because they are neither matters of "life and death" nor would they lead to the complete failure of your organization.

For these functions, there comes a point in time where work must resume.

However, this resumption is often by degrees. In other words, you don't simply have an interruption and then return straight to business as usual.

Instead the recovery life cycle is more likely something like this:

1. You have an outage.

2. You experience a period of interruption while recovery activities are undertaken.

3. You deploy some manual workarounds while services are suspended, and you wait for them to be recovered.

4. You recover basic services and operate at a reduced level of service, focusing on critical activities.

5. You clear backlogs and complete recovery of noncritical services and resources.

6. You return to normal operations.

Figure 6-1 illustrates this life cycle and breaks down the phases.

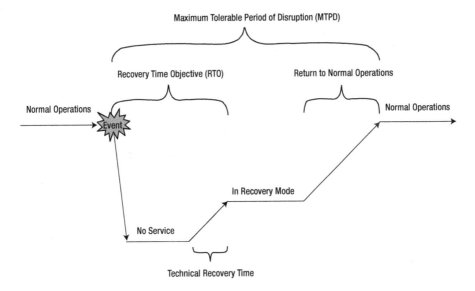

Figure 6-1. Business interruption and recovery diagram

Employ Manual Workarounds

These are alternatives practices, processes, and procedures that can be deployed while systems, suppliers, or other resources are unavailable. These are often quite basic activities, such as recording all customer queries on call sheets for investigation once systems become available again.

They are not designed to replace the normal processes but just to allow the most critical activities to keep going.

Size Your Solution

It's normal to size recovery solutions with adequate resources to maintain critical activities for the duration of an outage. That means you wouldn't, in most cases, size your recovery the same as your business-as-usual operation. The reason is simple: cost.

The aim here is survival first, and you are hoping that you'll never have to recover. What you shouldn't do, however, is gamble on the viability of your business. Spend the money you need to ensure a disaster doesn't put you out of business.

In most cases, you should be planning for running a reduced service during any business outage. You may have only half the staff able to work consequently, so you'll want to focus on critical activities only. For example, you decide to suspend all outbound sales activities and focus totally on servicing existing customers.

Business Recovery Options

There are a range of strategies open to you for restoring operations, and they are not mutually exclusive. So, they can be mixed and matched as you feel appropriate.

The key strategies are as follows:

- Work transfer
- Displacement of noncritical functions or people
- Doubling up
- Split site
- Offshoring
- Work area recovery (WAR)
- Mutual aid

Selecting one or more of these options depends in part on your needs and budget. However, when you approach this question, don't think you have to pick one or the other.

You can choose a blended approach, where you employ, for example, some WAR, displacement, and work transfer. Together, they might make up your overall recovery strategy.

Let's look at each option in more detail.

Work Transfer

This strategy is about moving the work, not the people. For example, if customer service is critical and done from New York and events conspire to close the New York office, you keep operations running by transferring customer service to the New Jersey office.

This assumes that the people who normally work in New Jersey will do the work. You're not sending trained people; you're switching the tasks only.

Using this strategy raises the following issues:

- Something will have to give because unless you have significant spare capacity at another location, some work will not be done.

- You will need to cross-train people to make sure they are able to do the work.

- You will need to monitor skills. It's not enough just to cross-train; you have to make sure that skill sets are maintained over time and reflect current needs.

- You will need to make technology available to do the work; this means access to systems must be provided to the workforce at the switch site.

- Any unique resources will need to be made available at the switch site including materials, stationary access to support, suppliers, and so on.

None of these are insurmountable challenges, of course. You simply need to think through them and make the best choice for your situation.

Displacement of Staff

This means sending noncritical staff home so that critical staff can use their desks, phones, and so on.

Continuing the previous scenario, we would send noncritical people based in the New Jersey office home so that critical staff who normally work in New York can work from New Jersey using the desks, PCs, phones, and so on, of the displaced New Jersey workers.

This requires tracking and occasionally recategorizing noncritical staff because it's easy for a person or even department that was noncritical last year to be indispensable this year.

This strategy is also hard to test because you will need to displace people and possibly whole teams to prove it's viable.

Doubling Up

This is where you use available desks and equipment in shifts. For example, one crew works from 8 a.m. to 4 p.m., and then another crew comes in to work in the same space from 4 p.m. until midnight.

To make this work, you could switch non-time-bound activities such as management reporting, research, development, and so forth, to the off-hours. For instance, your IT developers could work evenings, while IT support people work regular office hours when customers need them to be in.

This can leverage the available desks in WAR and significantly reduce your costs.

You can also use the strategy with existing desks at unaffected locations. For example, if equity research professionals have been affected by an incident that keeps them out of their offices, they could use the equity traders' desks when the markets are closed.

Again, doubling up desks requires that you monitor who is where, and it also raises issues around making the necessary technology available for different people at the same desk. It probably won't be practical to build a PC desktop for an equity research analyst every night and then rebuild the original desktop for the equity trader next morning. In this case, it's likely that the trader will have access to many of the same systems, and the additional reference sites may be Internet based.

Split Site

This is a mitigation strategy in which you may decide that something is so critical that you will split the workload between two sites—and at all times, not just during recovery. In effect, you ensure that all activities are replicated, and if one site is unavailable, the remaining site can pick up the corresponding workload.

This requires monitoring and strong management because the original drivers for a split-site strategy can be forgotten over time. Beware of one-off activities that start creeping in at one site and not the other. Also, you might start to see skills diminishing.

You also need to factor in that you will probably be able to undertake critical workload with only one site out. So again, this needs some clear thinking about exactly what you are going to do and also what you're not going to do.

Operating split sites is often the chosen strategy when work is offshored. However, while this is viable when work is split between onshore and offshore locations, it's generally the rule that once savings start to be delivered and the offshore partner gets experience, then the onshore capacity is reduced or goes away altogether.

Offshoring

Where there is offshore capacity, it is possible to switch onshore work offshore as long as the skills and access to technology and resources are available.

You have to consider what the impact will be on existing offshore work. However, you may find that there is more spare capacity than onshore, and they can quickly ramp numbers offshore by adding extra head count and desks or employing double seating.

Work Area Recovery

WAR is about providing an alternative workspace to operate critical functions. It's known by various names besides WAR, most notably *workplace recovery*.

This is normally provided by specialist vendors, and they have two types of offering:

- Dedicated
- Syndicated or shared

Of course, WAR can be provided in-house, and it can be a good way of using some spare capacity that you may have in your company's real estate portfolio.

However, if you do it in-house, you need to maintain the site to professional standards and ensure that you "ring fence" it from normal business use. Otherwise, you will end up with the site being used by business units over time, and once they are in, you will find difficult to shift them in a disaster. The other thing is that, while you start by just putting in project teams and noncritical people into the WAR site, over time these become more settled and critical. When you displace them because of a disaster or incident, you may find that this has a detrimental effect on your business.

The big advantage of the in-house WAR solution is that you will have access to the site 24/7/365 at no cost. You can also share it with all your locations at no extra cost.

Yet of course there is a cost to maintaining your own WAR even if a bill does not arrive in the mail. Maintaining a building for WAR is very expensive, and unless you can find a way to leverage it, the costs will be far higher than contracting it to a third party. Plus, you will have maintenance, cleaning, guarding, and more to take care of.

Syndicated WAR Contracts

There are many vendors who will provide space on demand. However, syndicated or shared seats are not sold for your exclusive use. The vendor will sell the same seats many times with certain restrictions designed to work in your favor.

Typical restrictions include the following:

- Geographic exclusion zones.

- The number of times that the seats will be sold.

- The seats can be used only for a disaster that impacts the contracted location.

In other words, they will not sell the same seat to two companies that are within the same geographical area (as defined in the contract). They will not sell the seats to more than, say, 20 companies, and you can invoke the seat only for an event that effects the contracted location.

These restrictions are in place to protect your risk and allow you to judge the viability of the recovery solution that you are contracting for. This is not obvious at first, but if a company contracts a WAR seat and then internally syndicates it for ten buildings, the chances of the seat being in use when you need it are significantly higher.

Shared WAR seats also come with greater restrictions when it comes to testing. Typically, you are allowed only one test slot per year.

There may also be restrictions on invocation. What happens if someone else has already invoked their need for the space? Clearly shared seats come with a significant risk because when you come to use them, they may already be in use. You won't be able to invoke the contracted seats. This is why it's so important that you assess these risks and make an informed decision.

Dedicated WAR Contracts

Dedicated seats mean that the vendor dedicates seats for your use only. This of course comes at a significant premium over shared seats.

Dedicated seats are necessary where you must guarantee that recovery seats will be available, when you need instant or frequent access to the recovery facility, or where you have unique technology requirements that need to be permanently deployed.

Dedicated seats are common among high-value businesses and critical infrastructure such as investment banks and utilities. Typically with investment banks, the amount of lost income, impact on their reputation, and market impact are such that dedicated recovery seats are not optional.

WAR Seat Allocation

Seats are normally allocated in accordance with the sizes of the suites where they are. This is commonsense from the vendor's point of view, on the basis that it's not practical or sometimes technologically viable to invoke two businesses into the same office space. From a commercial perspective, it wouldn't make sense to sell a few seats from a suite because it would preclude them from selling all of them to someone else.

However, for shared seats, exactly how the seats are allocated at the time of invocation varies depending on the vendor's chosen approach.

There are two approaches:

- First come, first served
- Equitable share

There are rarely negotiable. Once a seat is sold on a given basis, all subsequent seats at that site must align with these terms.

Note From time to time, WAR vendors will change their terms and introduce sitewide changes for all clients. This normally happens only when two vendors merge and then try to migrate clients with different contracts into the site. When this occurs, keep your eyes and ears open for changes that affect your plans.

First Come, First Served

This is literally the case: the first business that declares an invocation gets all their contracted seats, or at least as many as they need for the given scenario.

This highlights a major risk that when you need your WAR seats, they are not available. This is a very real risk because companies often find themselves needing to invoke their WAR arrangements.

To mitigate this risk, WAR vendors make a number of provisions. You will need to weigh these when selecting a vendor.

The main options are as follows:

- Use another suite in the same building; this is an option if the vendor has more suites and you have subscribed to a minority of available seats.

- Fall back to another WAR site. Most vendors have multiple sites and have the capability to deploy your recovery positions at a secondary site. This may introduce major logistical issues in terms of getting staff to the secondary site, but it is better than no site!

Equitable Share

This strategy relies on sharing seats between any businesses that need to use the available WAR seats. For example, if there are 200 seats arranged in 2 suites of 100, and 2 companies invoke that subscribe for 200 seats, they will get 100 each.

This raises a number of issues:

- What if there's only one suite? Can you work alongside another company?

- Can the vendor support concurrent invocations?

- What if the invocations are staggered? For example, say the first company has already fully invoked their need for space and then you invoke it later. Do they have to give up some of their positions?

- How are amicable agreements going to be reached quickly at times of crisis?

- When do you draw the line? What if, for example, three businesses invoked, or what if the available seats equate to less than 50 percent of what is contracted?

Again, all these potential challenges should be considered and thought through fully with contingency plans in place if things don't work out as planned or contracted for.

Setting Up Work Area Recovery

In normal operations, it's not unusual for everyone to have their own unique build, with just the applications each person uses.

I'd recommend that for your WAR solution, you adopt a generic build in which all the desktops have all the applications. This will simplify both the invocation and the ongoing maintenance.

If you have unique builds for every user, you will have to track every change and continuously update the builds. If you have generic builds, you need to change the build only when an application is introduced or changed.

You may find that licensing costs make this impractical, in which case I recommend having multiple generic builds, that is, a generic build for each department.

WAR INVOCATION RISKS

There are a number of invocation risks that need to be weighed when selecting a WAR vendor or indeed when deciding whether to do it in-house. These include the following:

- *Extended deployment*: WAR contracts cover you for a limited period that is normally 13 weeks. After this period, the vendor can kick you out. However, being business minded what actually happens is that your daily invocation fees go through the roof. So, this engenders two risks. First, you might lose the recovery site after the contracted period. Second, fees might rise to an unsustainable level.

- *Seats are in use when you need them*: It's not unrealistic to see that when you come to invoke your space either: someone has invoked already because of an earlier event, or someone affected by the same event as you has been quicker in invoking their contingency plans and consequently already secured the available seats.

- *Technology failure*: This is a high risk because technology changes quickly and is complex. It's quite easily mitigated by testing and introducing controls and processes that ensure that WAR solutions are maintained in parallel to your live environment. For example, if the production desktop builds change, then you will need to make sure that the WAR build is changed too—and tested before the release goes live.

Mutual Aid: Work with Suppliers and Competitors

Historically, many crises have been averted by working with competitors, other organizations that share suppliers, or the suppliers themselves.

If you are hoping that if it all goes terribly wrong someone else will come and bail you out, think again. Everyone will be looking out for themselves and their own organizations. However, sometimes cooperation is possible, and there may be a few organizations that could benefit from working with other organizations to get you through a crisis.

Typical examples might be to make spare capacity—be it raw materials, machine time, people, infrastructure, or facilities—available to another organization. For example, both you and a competitor might run your manufacturing at 75 percent capacity, so you might want to make some of the spare capacity available on a tit-for-tat basis. If you help someone out in a pinch, it's likely they will help you out when it's your turn to panic.

To make this work, you need to first identify suitable opportunities and then formalize the arrangement through a mutual aid agreement that sets out the conditions of the relationship.

Create a "Not Doing" List

There is generally too much focus on "what we will do," and this can often be overstated and naive.

So, I urge you to be clear about what you're *not* going to do.

Think through some basic scenarios: loss of technology, loss of site, unavailability of staff, denial of access, and loss of a key supplier. Then think through what you don't absolutely have to do, at least in the near term. After all, doing nothing, done right and strategically, can save you money without harming the business for the long term.

I'd make this formal if possible by getting whoever is accountable for the business activity to sign off on a statement that says, for example, that in a disaster, activities A, B, and C will be suspended. I'd also make sure that it's documented clearly in your business recovery plan.

This is a critical moderation step because it forces people to think through the deeper implications of suspending activities.

Know Your Recovery Solution in Depth

It's essential that you are clear about your current business recovery solution. In particular, you need answers to these questions:

1. What strategies will you use?
2. If you use WAR, is it dedicated or syndicated?
3. If it's syndicated, what is the syndication ratio, and how full is the site at this time?
4. If it's syndicated, is that on a "first come" or "equitable share" basis?

5. If it's "equitable share," how will this be decided and what restrictions exist?

6. What's the minimum number of seats you need to complete your critical obligations?

7. What fallback options does the vendor offer, and how viable are these for you?

8. If there's only one suite, can you work alongside another company?

9. Can the vendor support concurrent invocations?

10. What if the invocations are staggered, such as if the first company has already fully invoked and you invoke later. Do they have to give up some of their positions?

11. How are amicable agreements going to be reached quickly at times of crisis?

12. What testing has been done, and did it involve business unit users? Have you proven all the critical activities can be done at the recovery location?

13. How quickly can you resume operation from the recovery location?

14. If you have a split-site strategy or are planning to switch work, you will have to discontinue some work. What will be stopped, and is doing so realistic and? How long can you not do something before it becomes a disaster in and of itself?

15. Is adequate training undertaken, and is the staff experienced enough to support a split site or switching strategy?

16. Is monitoring of skills being undertaken?

17. Is access to all the required systems available to the workforce at the switch or split site?

18. Are there adequate change controls in place to maintain all technology in support of the chosen strategy?

19. How long is it viable to remain in the recovery location?

20. How will the return to normal operations be undertaken?

21. If a return to normal operations is not possible at the original site, can a new or temporary location be sourced before you exhaust the capacity of the recovery strategy?

22. Can all the required resources be made available at the switch site, including materials, stationary access to support, suppliers, and so on?

Remediation: Identify Gaps in the Plan

When you review your current situation, you may decide that you have some gaps. Maybe you need to extend or strengthen your strategy. Maybe you need to replace it.

The answer will require a project to deliver the necessary capability.

Build Business Recovery Solutions

The elements that make up a business recovery project are pretty similar to those described in the previous chapter on disaster recovery.

In short, the project must have the following: defined goals, deliverables, and a starting point and an end point. Also, regardless of what type of project it is, it will have the following steps:

1. Set out the requirements.
2. Evaluate the possible solutions.
3. Select the solution.
4. Create a detailed design.
5. Build.
6. Test.
7. Implement.
8. Sign off/close down.

The business case should fall within these steps, but exactly how you go about the project will be driven by your organization's process.

In all probability, you will not be the project manager, but you're not off the hook! You need to ask lots of questions to make sure the basics get done. A good starter list of ten basics follows:

1. Make sure that all the steps in the previous list are included.

2. Make sure the project is formalized, meaning that it is documented, with an agreed-upon schedule of work, allocated resources, identified risks and issues, regular progress reports, clear ownership of the project, and responsibility for managing the work.

3. Make sure the solution will meet your business requirements. For example, if the business has to be recovered in 4 hours, how will this be achieved, and what reasons do you have to believe this is possible?

4. Make sure you understand the solution that is being proposed. If you don't understand it, something is probably wrong. In general, this is pretty simple stuff—so the fault here is not with you for not understanding. However, it might be with whoever is explaining it to you.

5. Keep asking the simple questions:

    a. What?

    b. When?

    c. Why?

    d. How?

    e. Who?

6. Keep at it, and don't ever feel stupid for asking questions or intimidated. If you ask and still don't understand, ask again and again and again.

7. Another good question, if people bombard you with noise and technobabble, is "So what?" You'd be surprised how after a few iterations of "Yes, but so what?" you can quickly discover that you're about to pay for a platinum-plated doodad when you just need a no-thrills solution.

8. Make it your responsibility to sign off on the deliverables against the detailed design and functional requirements. That way, you can be sure that the requirements are being met.

9. Make sure people know at the outset that you're going to need to sign off on the deliverables before they can hand it over.

10. Understand why the final solution was chosen, why the others were rejected, and what compromises have been made. Will all the requirements be met, and is that acceptable? Has the accountable person been made aware and agreed to this decision?

Prepare a Business Continuity Business Case

Again, you'll probably need to prepare or at the very least, contribute, to a business case. Here are a couple of things I recommend you consider when you approach the business case:

- *Consult finance and get direction on exactly what goes into a winning business case.* You really don't want to keep going back and forward—get it right first time!

- *Identify any mandatory requirements and make these the focus.* For example, you may be contractually obliged to have business continuity for some functions.

- *Decide what constitutes an acceptable level of residual risk.* In other words, how much risk is acceptable after the project? When doing this, you need to make sure this is consistent with the risk appetite of your organization.

- *Assess a range of solutions and select the one that matches the risk appetite.*

- *Identify the ongoing running costs of the solution and factor these in.*

- *Don't wait until you submit the business case for it to see the light of day.* Make sure that all the key people who will be deciding on it are aware of what's in it and have bought into it. Obviously, decision day is not the day to be educating people on the finer points of your business case, so get out there in good time, speak to people, take their input on board, and go back to them until you can get them to say "yes." Once you are sure, then you can formally submit it for approval!

> ▬ **Tip**   Make the process of getting your case for business continuity approved a no-brainer. Do a thorough job, speak to finance, and get the guidance you need so you present your case in the desired format. Last but not least, engage all the stakeholders, gather their input, and secure their support before the case gets submitted for approval.

Release Solutions into the "Live" Environment

How you will implement the plan is a critical consideration. Again, just like DR, if you don't manage to transition to live with appropriate rigor, you will pay for it later.

Making sure the recovery solution works shouldn't be an objective. It should work because you should have tested it by now.

Instead, the key objectives here are as follows:

- Making sure the solution is documented.

- Making sure that support responsibility is defined.

- Making sure there is adequate funding to cover ongoing testing and maintenance work is budgeted.

- Making sure that your new solution is directly linked to the business it covers. For example, if the business materially changes, your business continuity solutions must be changed and tested too.

- Making sure any impacted business continuity plans must have been updated.

All this should be covered by the policies that cover business continuity.

Action Plan

Please take a little time to review these questions and think about the recommendations before moving on:

1. Are you clear about which functions need resilience as opposed to business recovery? If not, then review "Understand Resilient Functions."

2. Have you identified manual workarounds that can be deployed to deliver essential activities while the function is interrupted? If not, review the section on "Employ Manual Workarounds" to see whether this is relevant.

3. Have you reviewed your business recovery strategy, such as WAR, work transfer, and so on? If not, review "Business Recovery Options."

4. Have you identified all the activities that you'd suspend if you have to operate in recovery mode for a period of time? If you have, have you shared this with the affected areas and secured formal approval of the corresponding "Stop doing" list? If not, pull together a "Stop doing" list and get it signed off.

5. Have you achieved a comprehensive understanding of your existing business recovery capability? If not, review the questions you find in the section "Know Your Recovery Solution in Depth"

6. Do you have enough funding to both support new recovery solutions and maintain your business as usual activities? If not, then review the section "Prepare a Business Continuity Business Case."

7. Do new recovery solutions get properly tested and documented before going live? If not, then look at your change processes and consider some controls or gateways that would restrict future solutions being delivered that are not proven. If you're unsure, review the section "Release Solutions."

Supply Chain

Managing Supply Chain Continuity

With so many businesses depending on third parties to provide critical services, products, or resources, it's increasingly important to make sure the businesses that support your operations have adequate contingency arrangements. You need to be sure they can continue to deliver your services if they experience a disaster. You also need to know whether alternative suppliers are available and, if not, how you will cope with a supply chain failure. This chapter explores these concerns and sets out some simple actions that will expose the risks and make sure you get them covered.

Have a Plan in Place

It's almost a statement of the blinding obvious, but you need to plan for the interruption of the supply of goods and services that third-party organizations supply you.

Planning has two aspects. The first aspect is to plan for the failure of supply. This, in fact, should be one of your principal planning scenarios. Identify third parties that the business depends on, and then identify any workarounds in the event the supplier is unable to deliver the needed goods or services. Doing so helps you deal with the issue of supply chain risk from the bottom up.

The second aspect is mitigating supplier risk before disaster strikes; this is the top-down approach. First, identify which suppliers are critical; then, ensure that each one has solid contingency plans and resilience in place to ensure a smooth flow of goods and services to you or your customers.

For most critical suppliers, or where alternative supplies are hard to source, you may want to have a strategic plan that deals with a supplier's failure. This may go as far as switching to suppliers with solid risk mitigation plans in place or ensuring that you're not dependent on a single source of supply.

Assessing Third-Party Risk

Before going further, let's be clear about risk. Just because another company is doing something for you, the risk of failure is never transferred to them. Think about it—the supplier risks failing to deliver to a client, but you, on the other hand, risk losing your whole business.

This is an increasingly important issue as companies continue to outsource or offshore noncore activities to third parties.

Note   If you depend on suppliers for key inputs, you are the one at risk if any of them fails. That should give you more impetus to investigate your suppliers' DR and business continuity plans before putting a lot of trust into their operations.

First, Who Are You Dependent On?

You first need to understand exactly who you depend on and for what. The most thorough way to do this is to include a section in your business impact analysis that does the following:

- Identifies your critical suppliers
- Describes the services, products, information, resources, and so on, they supply you with
- Analyzes the impact on you if the supplier fails
- Describes possible internal workarounds
- Identifies alternative suppliers

Take time into consideration as well. Look at each supplier and ask what the impact would be if it is unavailable for 2 hours, 4 hours, 12 hours, 1 day, 2 days, 1 week, and 1 month. Some, you'll find, are more critical than others. One supplier, for example, may provide 24/7 technical services that you essentially can't do without at any time. Another might make a monthly delivery of noncritical items.

Make the Risks Visible

Creating this view will help you rank your suppliers in terms of critical-ity. Make sure you share this ranking directly with the salient parties, such as your steering committee, supply management executives, procurement professionals, and so on, and get it ratified before putting it into any formal plans or reports.

Big Picture and Focus

Remember, until you investigate, you know only which suppliers have the potential to cause you the most pain. You don't know any facts. You might find, for example, that the big exposures are all covered because they are mature organizations that have mature business continuity plans of their own. You are likely to find, however, that among the middle and lower tier of suppliers you might have the greatest risk. Many such firms have little or poor DR and business continuity plans.

Either way, you probably have quite a long list with a lot of gaps in terms of your knowledge of their actual capability.

I recommend that rather than working through them all, you split up the list and focus on the most critical suppliers first. There is going to be a significant number of suppliers that fall into the "not critical" category, such as paper goods suppliers, landscape gardeners, and so on. Make sure these are identi-fied so you can focus only on the critical suppliers.

Tackle the remaining list of suppliers in two phases. First, ask very high-level questions by sending out a simple questionnaire that helps you identify some basic facts and gives a sense of their capabilities.

The survey would ask high-level questions such as the following:

- Do you have a business continuity plan that covers the delivery of our service?

- Have you tested it?

- Do you have DR plans for IT systems that are required to deliver our service?

- Have you tested the DR plan for these systems in the last 12 months?

- If you had an outage that affected the delivery of our service, how quickly would the service be restored?

Having gathered more detail about your supply chain, next undertake a second phase where you can do a deeper dive—called an *individual assessment*—on the suppliers that are clearly most critical or represent the greatest risk.

In subsequent phases, you can expand the number of suppliers that you subject to a deep dive.

Individual Supplier Assessments

In these assessments, you need to expand the high-level questions to cover broader issues of governance and quality and then ask for evidence. So, for example, you will want to know about the following:

- Their BCM policy
- Accountability
- Crisis and incident management policies
- Testing schedules
- Access to test results

Remediation of Risks

You may unearth some significant issues where your suppliers don't have adequate continuity. In these cases, you'll need to document the issue, agree on an action, make sure it's owned, and monitor progress.

Business Continuity and Contracts

There's a good chance that up until now you have not adequately covered business continuity in your third-party contracts. For this reason, make sure that all new contracts include business continuity going forward.

This should not just be about the next contract. It's far better to look at the overall contract process and make sure you make changes to the contract process itself so that all future contracts consider business continuity.

On one level, this needs to be covered by standard terms and conditions. However, every supplier relationship is unique and has its own risks. Consequently, it's important that not only do you have suitable wording, but that you have personally been engaged in the process to review the assessment of the risks and how it is planned to be managed or mitigated to be sure that you're not just signing up to words or something that doesn't actually meet your needs.

The backbone of any contract has to be a clear definition of the levels of service and availability that you expect from the supplier and the maximum disruption time that is acceptable. This is fine when it's a new service that you are procuring, but where there are existing relationships in place, what do you do? In simple terms, make sure that when each contract comes to a contract break or for renewal, you review the contracts and supplier both to make sure that business continuity is adequately covered.

Tip Write into all contracts with suppliers that they must have business continuity plans in place. Be specific about service levels required and maximum disruption times. And don't trust their word that they have contingency plans. Ask for evidence.

Action Plan

Before moving on, reflect on the following questions and the corresponding recommendations:

1. Does your existing business continuity planning cover supplier failure? If not, then review all plans with this scenario in mind and suitable workarounds made. Where there is not suitable alternatives to supplier failure, assess the risk and take steps to raise the gap with crisis managers and mitigate the risk.

2. Have you identified all of your critical suppliers? If not, pull together a list of all suppliers and rank them by criticality.

3. Do you know if each supplier meets your business requirements? If not, find out by conducting supplier surveys to establish if they have adequate plans, if plans have been successfully tested, and so on.

4. Have you recorded all your risks and issues, have they been suitably escalated, and do you have appropriate actions plans agreed and underway?

5. Have you included business continuity in your new contract process?

6. Is anyone with business continuity experience engaged in the new contract process to review requirements, contracts, and supplier capability?

7. Make sure that as contracts come up for renewal or a contract break, business continuity is reviewed and contracts changed to reflect your new requirements.

Continuity Suppliers

Select and Manage Business Continuity Service Providers

If you rely on third parties to deliver business continuity or disaster recovery (DR), this chapter explains how to select the right partner and make sure that what they deliver matches what you need.

Selecting Business Continuity Suppliers

Choosing the right supplier is important because in a sense you are betting your business on them. It's also important because you will be locked into a relationship with them for the next 5 years or so.

The services in question fall into the following broad categories: business recovery (work area recovery [WAR]), technology recovery (IT DR), consultancy, and tools. There are suppliers that specialize in a small niche like crisis management or telephony recovery, and there are others that provide all the services and products.

■ **Note** Historically, large organizations conducted recovery activities in-house, but over time specialist organizations have sprung up, and their offerings have matured to the point where they are better than what can be offered in-house. Plus, they can be delivered quicker and at a lower cost.

Start with Your Needs

It can be a big mistake to start talking to suppliers before you have quantified your needs.

In the case of WAR, you should know the following:

- Locations that need to be covered
- Recovery times
- Approximate numbers of seats
- Technology, including desktops, servers, network connectivity
- Telephony, including voice recording, headsets, number of DDIs, fax, IVR, and so on

In the case of IT DR, you should know the following:

- Hardware
- Backups
- Networks including firewalls and routers
- Recovery time objectives
- Recovery point objectives

In the case of both WAR and IT DR you should also think about basic needs, such as security for the site, cleaning, refreshments, meeting rooms, and so on.

In the case of consultancy, you should know the following:

- What is the problem?
- When does it need to be solved by?
- How much is it costing you now?
- What must any consultancy engagement deliver?

In the case of tools, you should know the following:

- Target user group
- How many users
- Deployment restrictions such as hosting, platforms, cross-border data, and so on

I use this information to create a request for tender document that I pass to a short list of potential suppliers. (You should use whatever is the standard procurement documents and process mandated by your organization.)

■ **Tip** To find business continuity and DR service suppliers, simply search on Google for the keywords that interest you, such as *business continuity software*. However, I use this to just do some background research to get a feel for products and features. Then I take my time to go and talk to people who already use these services. The best place to start is your industry interest groups. You may find that someone has already undertaken a study, but people are always happy to tell you about their good and bad experiences.

Create on Objective View

Next, create a "vendor assessment" spreadsheet with all your requirements on it. Distinguish between mandatory requirements and those that are merely important. Apply a weighting to each requirement so that you can come up with an objective score for each supplier.

Make appointments to meet with providers and get answers and data to fill in your spreadsheet. I manage engagements with suppliers so that each gets the same opportunity to impress me. I normally have an initial meeting at my site to discuss the requirements, and then I give them an opportunity to gather more information that will help with their proposal. Next, I undertake site visits, making sure I visit all the proposed locations. At the end of each visit, I complete a vendor assessment.

I also like to work with at least two other key stakeholders on this, normally IT networking people, along with business representatives. I find they will have a different perspective on many aspects of the vendor and the proposed solutions. This generally proves fruitful, and I normally find things I'd otherwise miss.

■ **Tip** Bring IT and department managers along with you on site visits. They will have insights about what's needed and spot things you might otherwise miss.

Finally, it's down to the assessments. Sometimes, you can use this to whittle down the numbers of prospective vendors before undertaking a final round of selection. Even better, you might be able to make a choice at this point.

If I find that I or one of the other stakeholders is disagreeing with the choice, I always take some time out to review the issues. Spreadsheets are good but never perfect, and it could be that your criteria are wrong or you have missed something that turns out to be more important. It could also be something totally intangible, such as you don't like the supplier! Whatever the objection is, get to the bottom of it!

Contracts

Contracts are normally drafted by the supplier, but it's normally an iterative process where, based on the basic requirements, they will offer a draft contract for you to review. You will normally engage all the key stakeholders in your organization to go through the contract line by line with your lawyers to make sure you understand the contract and it aligns with the requirements and your internal standards. I normally have a behind-closed-doors review within the organization. Then, once we are clear about what issues or questions we have, we normally repeat it with the supplier and their legal team. This normally takes a couple of iterations and can be quite painful because the detail can be quite obtuse and dull. However, you should never treat this step lightly because you're committing your organization to a long-term relationship and financial liability.

First and foremost, before contracts are drafted, you need a clear definition of the following:

- The service
- How it will be measured
- What the penalties will be if the supplier fails to meet the agreed level of service

If you and the supplier are not clear on these points, you will be fighting an uphill battle when it comes to managing the service.

That means you should be actively involved in the contract negotiations.

If contract negotiations have already been completed and the contract is already in place, plan how you can get it sorted out. Find out when the next service review meeting is and make sure you get this tabled through whoever owns the relationship with the supplier.

You'll almost certainly hit a wall, in which case keep pushing, but also look to the next break clause in the contract or when it's due for renewal.

Either way, get the issue documented and owned and keep a focus on it, even if you aren't the one who will own it or ultimately resolve it!

Contract Breakpoints

Make sure you have breakpoints included in any contracts, and be aware of when they are coming so that you can table any changes in good time.

It sounds cynical, but you will find suppliers more flexible when there is an immediate threat to their ongoing income!

Contract Termination

Be mindful of the end of contracts for two reasons.

First, you need to allow yourself plenty of time to get the best possible deal with a new supplier. This means some planning, requirements gathering, testing the market, and a formal supplier selection process.

Second, if you have multiple contracts in place with different vendors, you should aim to co-terminate them and negotiate a single-supplier deal. It will make your negotiations more effective, because you'll have more leverage and should be able to get a better commercial deal. There's also significant reduction in overhead cost for you if you have to manage only one relationship. Overall, your operations are improved because each vendor will have a unique process for everything and idiosyncrasies within the service offering. It's often worth waiting longer so that you can get out of all your existing relationships. You'll get a better deal benefit over the long term from reduced cost and a simplified process.

KPI and Service Credits

Take time to understand the essentials that the continuity service provider must offer.

Think about this from the following points of view:

- Operational
- Customer
- Financial
- Legal
- Regulatory
- Employee

These generally relate to the same features or elements of the service but from a different point of view. Typically, this would include the technology and infrastructure such as data and telephony, as well as facilities and related services such as security, cleaning, and catering. There are also requirements around the facilities offering covering things such as size of suites, ability to segregate some teams, provision of meeting rooms, teleconference rooms, post rooms, and so on. Each of the previous may have a different view of each aspect of the service.

For example, if we think about suite size, operational requirements might be met by a large suite because it's easy for people to interact with all the people they work with. From a financial point of view, it might be good because it keeps costs down, but from a regulatory point of view it doesn't allow you to segregate some activities from the rest. And from an employee point of view, a large suite is not ideal; it's too noisy and busy, which makes it harder to work.

Try to formulate these requirements in measurable terms. These measurements will become your key performance indicators (KPIs) that tell you that everything is good and, if not, where you need to direct management attention.

For example, "Telephony will be available on all desktops within 1 hour of invocation, and fully imaged and working desktops will be available within 2 hours." Such requirements may already be documented as part of the original request for tender or whatever documents your organization uses.

Once you have identified the KPIs for each area, look beyond the essentials to the merely important and analyze them from the perspectives mentioned earlier.

Some of the requirements are obvious and relate to the immediate delivery of the critical services. Others are more mundane, but things such as having the soda machines cleaned and replenished become significant when you have to spend weeks at a recovery site.

Within your organization, you may have specialists who are dedicated to setting up and managing such agreements, but you still need to be aware of progress and drive it when necessary.

The specialists in third-party contracts and management probably won't be able to set the requirements, but they can help you pull them together and document them so that they can become part of the contract.

One area where they will be essential is in creating service credits. This is where you formulate the consequences of a failure to meet the KPIs. The penalty is normally financial, and it will be deducted from future payments. In practice, this may be more than offset by additional work that you will need from the supplier that's outside of the contract, such as extra test days, additional racking, and so on.

Service Reviews

You need to meet with the supplier about once a quarter, though an annual meeting might be good enough. You should review agreements in light of organizational changes and the volume of work you continue to do using the supplier.

Have a standard agenda along the following lines:

- Review previous minutes
- KPIs/service credits
- Issues
- Next test
- Planned work
- Any other business

Tests and Test Reviews

If you use third-party suppliers, then it's essential that when you test, you fully engage them in the design of the test and resolution of any issues. These should not be limited to just the technical aspects of the service; you should also measure the customer experience of using the service and feed that back, too.

After the test, you should include a review of the suppliers' performance.

Formalize the review by including supplier KPIs in the test and producing a test report that gets sent to the supplier. Then review the results with the supplier and agree on improvements needed.

Few companies do this, but it's a great opportunity to build a better relationship with your supplier as you're giving them valuable feedback and working with them to improve the service.

This is quite shocking. Just recently, I was talking to the managing director of the United Kingdom's largest business continuity firm, and he said that only 40 percent of his clients tested their service. He's totally committed to testing because he knows it's the best way to get the service right and to be sure it will work at a time of crisis.

Demand Good Service

It's important to remember that you are the customer and you deserve the best service possible. If you feel you're not getting a good service, challenge the supplier.

It's really important you have a good relationship with the supplier; it makes for a better service and a better life. The key to this is the quality of the person who looks after your account. I've made the mistake in the past of judging the supplier by the account manager. This can be a costly mistake because you can become so disillusioned that you jump ship to a new supplier, which comes at quite a cost for changing and may not offer a better service. Really, it wasn't the supplier that needed to change; it was the account manager.

■ **Tip** If you find that you're unhappy with the service that your account manager for the continuity service is giving you or you don't have a good relationship, demand a new account manager.

This improves matters on a few different levels. First, it removes an issue of concern; second, it keeps the next account manager on his toes; and third, it's good for the supplier if you get an account manager who is doing a great job as opposed to someone who is causing delays and irritating you, the client.

The difference between account managers is massive. I've had account managers who couldn't get anything done, failed to complete actions, and irritated my staff and their own. I've seen these "failures" replaced with people who could do wonders and made me feel that they were working for me as much if not more than for their own company.

Keep Suppliers Keen

You want to build a good and positive relationship with the supplier, and you should have a frank and fruitful working relationship with your account manager. But remember, you're not in this to be popular; you're doing it to look after your company's best interests.

The good news is that the best interests of both companies often overlap, but the bad news is that some suppliers or their salespeople will put their interests before yours so they get the maximum reward and you get the minimum service.

Yet don't be anything other than positive, have high expectations, and know the market, all so you can assess that you are getting a fair deal. If it's a fair deal, the supplier will make a reasonable margin, and you get good value and an offering that meets your needs. The best way to "know the market" is to have a dialogue with competitors and your peers. Try to access benchmarks for your industry or the service you are buying in.

If you're not getting a good deal, let the supplier know. Talking to other suppliers keeps them on their toes too, and when you come to renew, make sure you get competitive quotes.

The surest way to secure a great service with fair commercial terms is through your account manager. Remember, you are the customer. Be fair but clear, and if the account manager doesn't measure up, you know what to do!

Tip Get competitive quotes for third-party continuity services whenever a contract comes up for renewal. Even if you're happy, it'll keep your current supplier on its toes.

Action Plan

Have a look at the following questions and reflect on the resulting recommendations:

1. Do you have a clear set of business recovery requirements? If not, then you'll need to go back to the BIA and document RTOs and RPOs for every component that requires recovery. You will have to also capture technical requirements such as number of CPUs, amount of memory, and so on.

2. Do you have a clear set of business provider requirements? This covers the practical aspects of third-party solution: how far a recovery site can be from your office, how many tests a year you want to undertake, whether you need them to provide security, cleaning, and catering, and so on. When you set these out, make it clear, for you at least, whether requirements are mandatory, important, or nice to have, because this will make the scoring much easier when it comes to selection.

3. When selecting, do you assess prospective vendors consistently? Is this process easily audited? If not, then where is the inconsistency? Consider documenting a formal acquisition process and using scored assessments that can be used to compare and contrast different vendors.

4. Do you have standard terms and conditions that can be used? Do your contracts document all the elements of the service that you are contracting for? Are any additional costs or responsibilities clear? If not, get some professional help to review your contract.

5. Do you have KPIs in place with pre-agreed service credits if these KPIs are breached? If not, then I recommend investigating this approach and get some specialist advice on including them in your contract.

6. Do you perform regular service reviews with your suppliers? If not, then I recommend that you introduce them.

7. Do you review the supplier's performance following every test? If not, then I recommend making this a formal part of your test life cycle and provide them with a report where they sign off on the agreed actions.

8. Are you aware of the contract breakpoints and termination dates? If not, then find out when these breaks are, and start to think about how you should approach future commercial negotiations. Get advice from your organization's procurement or vendor management specialists if you have them.

9. Do you have a good commercial relationship with the supplier? Does your account manager seem to get things done for you, come back quickly, and so on? If not, then remember you are the customer and ask for a new account manager. If you find that the service is consistently bad, then factor this into the next round of negotiations. In other words, do you want to do business with a supplier that can't do the basics right?

Education and Awareness

How to Educate the Workforce

Having people who understand their responsibilities and are well versed in how to undertake them in a variety of stressful situations is essential if an organization is to survive a disaster or any other major out-of-the-ordinary event that upsets operations. This chapter will help you understand your education needs and deliver a program that prepares all key staff for potential disasters.

The Point of Education

Plans are important, but in reality, they are not essential. What's essential is having a capability that enables you to recover or able to improvise a recovery within the critical time frame. If you can't recover, then it's a distinct possibility that you will not have an organization after disaster strikes.

Similarly, having a technical recovery capability is only half the story. If you don't have people who can invoke the recovery and people who can adapt quickly as events change, then your recovery capability is useless.

Education and awareness are principally concerned with making sure people are prepared for the likely eventualities.

It will tell them what to do if they have a role to play. If they don't have a role, it will tell them what will happen to them, where they can get information during a disaster, and what they should do if any part of the organization is crippled.

Ideally, education and awareness should also root out any people who have been given roles they aren't suited to. This is never easy because most people refuse to accept their weaknesses and are even worse at pointing out weakness in others, especially if the person in question is someone in power.

Note Education and awareness, when it comes to business continuity, are all about preparing people for their roles in a disaster to ensure operations are affected as little as possible.

Before going further, let's be clear:

Education addresses people's need to attain skills and knowledge to perform specific recovery roles. It also affords them an opportunity to practice in a safe environment where they can make mistakes—and learn from them—without pressure.

Awareness is about raising everyone's awareness about business continuity. It's about making sure everyone in the organization knows what to expect, what they will need to do, and where they will need to be if a disaster arises.

Education and Awareness Program

Education and awareness activities are often grouped together in a single ongoing program of work.

Awareness Events

Awareness events are normally scheduled to take place throughout the year. There are many low-cost options for getting the word out. These include the following:

- *Team briefings and formal presentations*: You can join team meetings throughout the organization to give informal presentations. You can also stand up and deliver full, formal presentations at official town hall–type events. You may want to do these yourself, or you can provide the individual business continuity coordinators with a slide deck. If you delegate this, I recommend doing a "train the trainer" session first and attend as many as you can to judge quality and make improvements to future training sessions or materials.

- *Market stand*: From time to time there will be events that take place in your organization where you will have an opportunity to set up a stand and promote BCM.

- *Desk drops*: In a "desk drop," you leave fliers on all staff desks. Fliers typically cover things such as evacuation procedures, muster points, contact information, what to do in an event, and so on.

- *E-mails*: Here you might send out a pack of documents via e-mail. It's similar to the desk drop, but you rely on people opening attachments, printing out instructions, and so on.

- *Screen savers*: You can sometimes get a slide included for a while as the screen saver on all the company PCs.

- *Internal publications*: You might be able to include an article in an internal publication or newsletter. You'll often find that many areas have such publications, including HR, information security, IT, quality, and so on. They are often looking for suitable content to fill their newsletters and so will welcome your interest.

- *Quiz or competitions*: Don't laugh. One company I worked for struggled to get the business continuity message out, especially to junior administration staff. Then they did a competition with a Nintendo Wii (when it was a really hot commodity) as the prize. They asked people to read an article and answer some questions. They kept all the responses as evidence that they'd gotten the message out—and they nearly sank under the volume of responses. That was achieved for less than $250 as opposed to the thousands of dollars in man hours spent on less-fruitful tactics. The result was that within days, just about everyone in the head office had read and could repeat the information they needed to know about business continuity.

Tip Consider a quiz or competition of some sort to promote awareness of business continuity. All entries go into a drawing for something your people will find of value. You'll get a much better response than you expect.

Education Activity

Education tends to works best when it's responsive to specific needs. Generally as soon as someone assumes a new responsibility, they should be trained in the basics.

For example, when someone has been made the business continuity coordinator for the IT department, there is a very specific set of things they need to know about. Some of these things will be generic and common to all departments, such as what a business impact analysis (BIA) is, why we do it and how, and when to complete the BIA. Other things will be unique to their role. For example, IT may have two discreet challenges: first, to recover the technology in a disaster, and then, in addition to the recovery support they have to provide, they need to plan for the continuity of their business. Thus, they will have to continue to support all the critical services, mandatory change, and anything else identified as critical by the BIA. This focused approach to education where it's more tailored works well because people can see what's in it for them and it relates to their actual responsibilities.

Someone assuming new responsibilities for business continuity is a trigger event, and it needs to be the business's responsibility to organize training.

Also, when you have any new joiners, they should have a basic overview of business continuity that covers what it is, how it is managed, what to do if an event happens, and how to find out more information at times of crisis using things like a staff hotline, Internet page, or contact details.

The business continuity coordinator should brief all new joiners on the details of their business continuity plan and their role, if any, and provide details of the recovery site and how to get there.

It's advisable to have a rolling schedule of training events, such as annual training for business recovery coordinators. This can be timed to precede the annual DR test, or, if you have sufficient demand, you can have these repeated through the year. That way, as new coordinators are appointed, they can go on the next training event.

You should aim to get face to face with all key people—members of your crisis management team, for example—annually. Use this meeting as an opportunity to review the roles and responsibilities of each person. While you're doing this, you can focus on any areas they or you may feel is weak. If necessary, you can arrange a supplementary session to focus educating people in key positions who need extra help.

What Are Your Needs?

When I set up an ongoing education and awareness program, I always start by undertaking a survey of the educational needs of the organization. I start by preparing a basic questionnaire that covers the key areas of knowledge and do some sample surveys.

Typical questions include the following:

- Do you know whether you have any responsibilities in the event of a disaster?
- Do you know who your business continuity coordinator is?
- Do you know what the plan is for recovering your department in a disaster?
- Do you know how to find out information in a disaster?
- Do you know where your business recovery site is and how to get there?
- Do you know whether you have been allocated a seat at the recovery site?
- Have you ever been to the business recovery site?

You have to tailor the questionnaire to reflect your organization and the strategies you use. For example, if you don't have a recovery site but instead shift work to other locations, then this should be reflected in the questions.

You might also have some additional surveys for specialist areas such as IT, BCM specialists, and crisis management team members.

Here are the typical questions for a recovery coordinator:

- Do you know what you have to do in the event of a disaster?
- Do you know who your business continuity manager is?
- Are you comfortable with the BIA process? If not, what are you unsure about?
- Do you know when the BIA and business continuity plan (BCP) needs to be updated?
- Are you familiar with all sections of the BCP? If not, what are you unsure about?
- Do you know how to do desktop walk-throughs with your recovery team?

- Do you know what you have to tell a new joiner about business continuity?

- Do you know how to get changes to the BIA and business recovery plan (BRP) approved by your management?

- Do you know what you need to do to prepare for a contingency test, such as preparing test scripts or organizing attendees?

- Do you know what to do during a test, such as monitoring the correct completion of test scripts, gathering the completed test scripts before people leave, and escalating issues through the agreed-upon process?

- Do you know what you have to do after a test, such as logging any issues and making sure that they are appropriately escalated to management, reviewing the lessons learned, and making improvements to the BRP and any related materials?

Here are the typical questions for a crisis team member:

- Do you know what you have to do in the event of a disaster?

- Do you know who your business continuity manager is?

- Do you understand the criteria and process for convening the crisis team?

- Do you regularly maintain your crisis management documents?

- Are you familiar with the crisis plan? If not, what are you unsure about?

- Are you familiar with your unique responsibilities on the crisis team?

- Do you know how to conduct yourself in a crisis exercise?

Here are the typical questions for an IT recovery team member:

- Do you know what you have to do in the event of a disaster?

- Do you know who your business continuity manager is?

- Are you familiar with recovery scripts you will use in a disaster?

- Do you understand how business continuity integrates into your change management process?

- Do you know how to make changes to the recovery scripts and what the change controls are around such changes?

- Do you have the right skills to undertake your recovery tasks?

- Do you know what to do during a test, such as how and where to record timings, who to notify on completion of tasks, escalating issues through the agreed-upon process, and so on?

- Do you know what you have to do after a test, such as logging any issues and making sure that they are appropriately escalated to management, reviewing the lessons learned, and making improvements to the test script, recovery process, tools, and staff training?

Then, using the responses, focus the program to address the areas of greatest need. I apply a little common sense to focus first on those areas that are both gaps and represent the biggest risk. I also weigh the amount of effort involved as well so that I can make the maximum impact on education and awareness as quickly as possible.

Measuring Education and Awareness

I'm no genius and I definitely don't have divine insight, so I can't be sure that I know exactly what works and what doesn't. That's not a problem for me, and it shouldn't be for you. Don't be too hard on yourself. As a principle, I always expect some things not to work. That's life, and your job is to spot them and sort them out!

So, with my ego intact, even though I assume that I'm probably making some mistakes, I test everything that I think matters. In particular, I test whether the training and awareness events are having any impact.

This is generally as simple as repeating a sample of the earlier education survey questionnaire after the training and comparing the scores.

If the survey shows that you have not made the impact you may have hoped for, don't get hung up. Try to understand what you could do differently. It could be that the people being trained are very hands on, and giving them lots of things to read didn't work for them, so you need to make the training more experiential. If there are specific issues that can be tackled as a "one-off" training and are worth doing, do it. If not, include it in your plan for next year.

It doesn't mean that you're no good. In fact, it means that now you're better than you were because you know something—you know what doesn't work, and that is priceless! In essence, you've gone from being unconsciously incompetent to consciously incompetent, which is a step many people never manage.

■ **Tip** Don't assume people have been "educated." To ensure they have absorbed the message you want them to, test their knowledge before and after training. If you still see knowledge gaps, don't kick yourself; train some more.

Action Plan

Before moving on, reflect on the following questions and the corresponding recommendations:

1. Have you identified your education and awareness needs? If not, then I recommend doing a survey of what you need and formalizing the requirements.

2. Do you have a planned set of activities to deliver education and raise awareness? If not, then prepare a plan of what you're going to do, when, and with whom.

3. Do you keep records of what training and awareness has been delivered? If not, then start keeping records that will enable you to manage an effective and comprehensive ongoing education and awareness program.

4. Do you go back regularly and review how effective your education and awareness is? If not, then regularly assess the current state and have some KPIs that will tell you how you're doing and whether you need to take remedial action.

Governance and Reporting

Essentials for Business Continuity

This chapter presents what is essential when it comes to business continuity: making sure things are done to agreed-upon standards, understanding what challenges you might have with your practices, and knowing what routine tasks are required. This chapter covers policy, processes, the key reports, and how you can have all these without creating a bureaucracy that slows response time to disasters and other negative events.

Create a Policy

First, create a policy on business continuity. This should of course be consistent with your organization's standards for policies. However, the thing that is universal is the need to set out, at a high level, what it is that business continuity exists to achieve and who is responsible for the key aspects of it.

Note Two appendices in this book will be very helpful in crafting business continuity policies and governance structures: Appendix D: Resources and Contacts and Appendix J: Business Continuity Management Standards. In addition, you will find numerous policies relating to business continuity just by doing a simple Web search on the topic.

You could split your policy into a policy document and a set of standards or you could have a set of policies covering the range of disciplines that make up business continuity management, such as business continuity planning, IT service continuity, and crisis management.

In simple terms, any policy should contain:

- A set of objectives
- A statement of accountability
- A set of responsibilities

These should be described at a high level, but must be clear enough for you to manage business continuity across your organization.

Set Standards and Create Processes

Once you have a policy in place, you need to implement it. To do that, you should have something equivalent to a set of standards or a good practice guide that sets out specifically how you will undertake the objectives identified by the policy. You will also benefit from describing the lifecycle of business continuity activities and how these relate to one another.

Finally, you will need a program of work that is completed on an ongoing basis. This program makes sure the key activities that make up the process are completed regularly and to a consistent level of quality.

You can think of it as a hierarchy, as shown in Figure 10-1.

Figure 10-1. Governance hierarchy

Tip Don't put the cart before the horse. First, set policy. Then, create standards. Last, put events in motion and controls in place to ensure you can maintain business continuity in the face of a disaster.

Assign Steering and Management Accountability

The policy should define management accountability; ideally this will be delegated to an individual or individuals rather than, say, the "crisis team," because it's much easier to get traction when one person is held accountable.

This shouldn't be a passive role. The accountable manager or managers should be actively involved in strategic planning, aware of issues, and signing off on any new risks or changes.

A steering team meeting is a good idea. Normally, this will convene quarterly, and it should have a consistent agenda and be formally recorded.

A typical agenda would be:

- Strategy
- Progress against plans
- Issues
- Risks
- Update by location, business line, product, or asset class (use whichever is most relevant for you)
- IT disaster recovery update
- Work area recovery (WAR) update

Assess Maturity Annually

Some of the key responsibilities of the steering committee are to set the long-term strategy and to ratify the plans that will both deliver the strategy and deliver business-as-usual business continuity activities (assessments, walk-throughs, etc.).

Before you set out on any journey, you need to know where you are now. Furthermore, as you make progress with your plans, you need to keep checking the map to make sure you are on the right path.

A maturity assessment is a useful tool to achieve both of these tasks. These assessments don't need to be nearly as complex as they sound. You just need to identify some key controls for business continuity and then define some measures for each control. Finally, decide how each measure can be represented in terms of process maturity.

To illustrate this, take a single aspect of business continuity such as business impact analysis. A control might be something like "Every business unit has completed a business impact analysis within the past 12 months."

The following maturity model is recommended for self-assessment. You should be able to determine the level of adherence to the control objective either as self-assessment or independent review.

The scale used for the maturity model ranks from 0 to 5:

> 0: Nonexistent. Management processes are not applied at all.
>
> 1: Initial. Processes are ad hoc and disorganized.
>
> 2: Repeatable. Processes follow a regular pattern.
>
> 3: Defined. Processes are documented and communicated.
>
> 4: Managed. Processes are monitored and measured.
>
> 5: Optimized. Best practices are followed and automated.

The maturity model is used by conducting the following mappings and comparisons:

- The current status of the organization: where the organization is today.

- The current status of the industry (best in class in): the comparison.

- The organization's strategy for improvement: where the organization wants to be.

How many controls you have is up to you. These may already exist for your organization if, for example, you already have a control framework like COBIT (see Appendix J) in place.

Once you have assessed the controls, you can make some fundamental decisions about the level of maturity you want to achieve. You might not need to be fully mature in all the controls. Some may be mandatory and require immediate attention; the great thing about doing the maturity assessment is that you can start to make some informed decisions about where you'll focus attention.

You will also have a powerful tool when it comes to dealing with internal and external auditors.

Note   You don't need to achieve a maturity status of five for every control you place. Some will be more important than others and should receive your attention first.

Manage Information

The only meaningful management information is that which provides the necessary insight to direct management attention and action.

Specifically, you need to know:

- That you are compliant with the appropriate policies, standards, and controls.

- That all business-as-usual activities are being done on time and to standard.

- That any remediation actions are being completed on time.

- That when issues have emerged, actions have been suggested to address the issue, who is responsible, when it will be done, and how progress will be measured.

- When any risks that threaten business continuity appear.

- Any other information that affects strategic initiatives. If a strategic priority is to increase productivity of staff, for example, then you need to have some relevant measure of productivity for business continuity management staff, and those with BCM responsibilities, so you can demonstrate how you have supported the initiative.

Personally, I like to have a monthly meeting that covers these or similar topics. In my reporting, the focus is by exception—we focus on things that require management action. However, I also include a summary of key successes and milestones, as management should also have an opportunity to see and praise success and progress.

Audit Plans and Actions Regularly

Increasingly, audit is a key focus for those involved in business continuity, because managing business continuity increases in importance to the organization. In addition, more and more industries are becoming regulated and prescriptive, and business continuity is a common area of focus for industry regulators. Last but not least, it's increasingly common for business continuity to be a requirement of service suppliers as part of any contract that they may try to win.

For all these reasons it's essential that business continuity is set up properly and for you to be able to demonstrate good governance.

To this end, you need to have a robust framework that includes your policy, processes, procedures, tools, and documents. Critically, you need to be able to demonstrate that you not only have a framework, but also that you are following it.

In the real world, you're not perfect. That's normal, but what's important is that you know:

- Where you're not okay
- Where you are deviating from the framework or where it's not yet been implemented
- Where you can demonstrate gaps in your reporting

You also need to be able to show that:

- The appropriate people are aware of any gaps
- Appropriate and timely actions are planned to improve the situation

Audit—normally a separate function in only the larger companies—is wonderful. I can honestly say that almost everywhere I've worked is a better place for audit's presence. For me, audit refocuses away from the solution end of things to the overall framework, controls, strategy, and doing what I say!

Having said that, it can be galling at times when you have self-identified issues and then you find audit writing you up for them as though they had brought civilization to the new world.

Don't take it personally, but keep your eyes open and think about audit being somewhere on the horizon. Don't wait for the call; make sure that a big part of what you are doing day in and day out is improving the governance and controls that support business continuity.

Tip Plan to audit your business continuity plan, policies, standards, and controls regularly. You want to uncover problems before anyone else does.

Action Plan

Before moving on, reflect on the following questions and recommendations:

1. Do you have a policy that sets out overall business continuity objectives, accountability, and individual responsibilities? If not, then you'll need to create a policy that is consistent with your organization's standards.

2. Have you set some standards of quality for business continuity? If not, then you'll need to review everything in the policy and formalize what constitutes an adequate standard (e.g., "Call cascade updates will be completed annually.").

3. Are the key activities documented so they can be repeated to a consistent standard? If not, then you'll need to look at writing processes for the key activities.

4. Do you have an ongoing program of activity that is designed to ensure that your organization continues to meet the requirements of your policy? If not, then you'll need to think about creating one.

5. Are senior managers engaged in strategic planning, aware of issues, and signing off exposures? If not, then you'll need to think about how to engage them and manage their accountability. This might be done through a mixture of steering committees, one-on-one meetings, waivers, and exception reports.

6. Do you have an understanding of how mature your processes and capabilities are? Have you decided, for the key activities, what the target level of maturity should be? Do you have plans to achieve the target level of maturity? If not, then consider benchmarking or a similar process that will determine the current level of maturity and allow you to make some informed longer-term strategic decisions about where you want to go. It will also give you a key mechanism for understanding when you have actually achieved your targets.

7. Does management receive reports that inform them when they need to take action? If not, then you'll need to review your reporting. Note: the reason for providing reports is so management can identify issues and take appropriate action!

Test and Maintain Your Continuity and Recovery Plans

Testing Principles

Things You Need to Know About Testing

Once you have your plans and solutions, you have to make sure they will work. Testing is the principal way of doing this. However, testing has to be regular; most organizations and their technology change quickly. This chapter covers the reasons testing is so important, some of the most important testing principles, the tests you can administer, and the different scenarios you should test for.

Note This chapter goes over the fundamentals of testing and conducting exercises. Chapters 12 through 14 cover IT testing, business operations testing, and crisis management exercises, respectively, in depth.

Why Test?

The simple answer to the question "Why test?" is because business continuity, DR, and crisis management are all very complex and have a tendency not to work. This is particularly true if you haven't tested your plans before.

DR, WAR, and BCP Won't Work Without Testing—and Sometimes Not Even Then

I'll explain the statement in this header further: In a quarter of a century of working in this field and having been involved in thousands of solutions that have been created by some of the smartest people on the planet, I suspect not a single one would have worked without incident if they had not been tested beforehand. If the brain trust can't get this right, would you bet your job, career, or life on the guys in your IT department or indeed yourself?

Further, just because your solution was tested doesn't mean it will work either. Just because you have a test status, a test report, or—worst of all—a RAG (red, amber, green) status that says everything is green, it doesn't mean all is well.

Don't be complacent.

That is the lesson I learned from acquiring other people's DR solutions after business mergers and acquisitions. Most of these inherited solutions came with test reports that said the solution had been tested and there were no major issues. However, when I tested the solutions for myself, they didn't work. And it's not because of changes that crept in since the last successful test. Many of these "solutions" would *never* have worked!

I can think of one bank that had a data center DR site that only had network links to the production data center it protected. So, if they'd lost the main data center, they could have brought up DR, but it would be invisible to the business in any scenario where the production site was down!

This sort of thing is quite common. I think it happens when people look at DR from the wrong perspective. A common error is thinking that having a standby location that replicates their production data center is enough. The solution in my example did that, and they had even tested recovering it (hence the "green status"), but in designing and testing their DR solution, they hadn't thought about using it in a disaster or tested that eventuality.

Things Change

Another reason why you need to have a routine testing regime is because things never stay the same.

As a result, I'd recommend two things:

- Test at least annually
- Make sure that any changes that affect DR or WAR are tested

What might affect DR and WAR? If you take a moment to think about the complexity of either one, you'll realize how easy it is for things to break down. You have environmental factors, hardware, operating systems, middleware, applications, databases, network connectivity, batch programs, administration suites, static data, external data feeds, business processes, suppliers, and users, to name just some of the things that can impair your recovery capability.

Things Are Dynamic!

I've already mentioned complexity. This should also highlight the fact that the exact situation you have tested is not likely to exist when you come to invoke a recovery.

At the most basic level, you may not be using exactly the same hardware, software, people, network, or suppliers as when you last tested. So be mindful of what you're actually testing and what you've actually proved. And don't panic. Keep it real and use the issue of complexity to keep regular testing at the top of your agenda.

■ **Tip** Don't get complacent. Just because your test worked last year doesn't mean it will work this year. It may not! The only way to truly be prepared is to test and refine your plans.

Pragmatic Testing

Although I advocate testing changes that impact DR, this is not always possible for a number of reasons:

- The availability of test slots: For example, you might have only one time a year when you can test, and you wouldn't want to put off all changes for up to a year.

- Risk: Testing is a risky activity, especially if you include live operations. In fact, the risk of the change failing and its consequent "potential" impact on your business can be far less than the risk associated with testing.

- Volume of change: Given the number of components that can impact DR and the frequency with which these can be changed, doing a full DR test for every change is neither practical nor sensible.

Clearly then, you need to be pragmatic and flexible. However, this flexibility must be exercised within the constraints of some basic principles. At the top of that list will be doing a full, end-to-end DR test at least once a year.

You Must Be a Realist

Before I proceed on the topic of testing, a word about an area that often throws sand in the gears of business continuity: the quest for perfectionism. We are cursed with perfectionism; managers in particular expect everything to be perfect. They don't accept imperfection, and all too often frown on bad news. This is both unrealistic and unwise. We live in a complex world; things rarely work out of the box.

Yes, we need to strive for the best possible solutions and maintain high standards. But, keep it real. Keep your eyes peeled for things that don't work or won't work.

Don't Shoot the Messenger

The cultural problem with perfectionism is that it creates a climate of fear. In general, people become afraid to make mistakes, so they don't try anything different and certainly don't take on any risks. Perhaps worse of all is that in this climate people stop reporting the truth. They tell managers what the managers want to hear.

In some cases the managers are overtly creating a culture of perfectionism. In two large firms I've personally experienced things that have frankly made my position untenable and forced me to look for another job.

First, I was told by a chief technology officer to change the "reds" on my report to "greens." At first, I thought, he wants me to fix the underlying problem. But he just meant change the report so this major exposure disappeared.

At another firm, a senior manager berated one of her staff for confirming when pressed by her boss in a meeting that he'd never seen a report. She actually told him that he should have said he had seen it and it was fine.

These weren't bad people; they were just under huge amounts of pressure. Make sure you don't stop the flow of bad news by being unrealistic and creating an atmosphere where people are too scared to be open and honest!

When people tell you things are bad or could be better, recognize this as the good news it is. Sure, it's not great if there's a fault, but better to know how things really are than to live in a fantasy world.

Fundamentally, this bad news actually means you've just moved from being "unconsciously incompetent" to "consciously incompetent." At last you know something now—you know what doesn't work. Armed with this insight, you can get on with sorting things out and making it work.

If someone is at fault, focus on what it is that they've done, accept it, and make sure they don't repeat the mistake.

A big part of the role of business continuity is to create a culture where the truth can flourish. Part of this is about making this clear to management and getting them to agree to it during your steering meetings or similar forums. It's hard in public for anyone to disagree with this point of view.

The other part is about evangelizing this to all the people doing the tests, especially IT staff, who often feel huge pressure not to have a "bad test."

What Testing Proves

You may have proven your test but have you proven you can recover from a disaster? This is quite a hard thing to take on board. By testing you have proven that the test works. You have not proven DR works unless you actually invoke it under duress.

Of course if your test involves live invocation, you're pretty much there! But you need to be mindful of the various different scenarios and how each might play out. This insight should have a deep impact on your behavior and on those you work with.

The implication is that you need to constantly keep looking at your testing from different angles. You should use this to create new scenarios to test.

Don't get me wrong; a successful test result is a big step toward having confidence in the viability of your plan, solution, and the preparedness of the staff to execute the plan.

I'd strongly recommend that you:

- Review scenarios every year. When considering new scenarios, think about the most likely scenarios first. Don't just repeat last year's test.

- Look beyond just technical recovery (i.e., just getting the system up). Make the tests progressively more complex, introducing more end-user involvement and if possible end-to-end processing.

- Look beyond live running in DR and start testing the return to production from DR.

People Expect You to Test

There is increasing pressure from auditors, regulators, customers, and even management to be able to provide evidence that you will be able to recover from an interruption to normal business.

Consequently, you have to be very methodical in your test approach. You need to create evidence of your efforts: the process for setting up the test, rationale behind the scenario, and how they fit into your broader strategy.

You must keep excellent records of the tests. Record exactly when events happened. You can use the resulting timeline to calculate the actual recovery time achieved during the test.

You need to be clear about the realism of your test results. It may take 4 hours to recover a system when you have just performed an orderly close down and have the right people ready to start with all the resources they need ready. That doesn't give you an accurate feel for how long it would take to recover the same system if it were halfway through the overnight batch or if it occurred on a normal day but none of the experts were immediately available.

You should also keep clear records of any issues that occurred during a test and how they were resolved, by whom, and when.

The Stakes Are High, So You Have to Get It Right

Never forget that the stakes are high when it comes to continuity. It's possible that if you fail to recover, then your business itself will most likely fail quite quickly afterward.

This isn't scaremongering; the research backs it up. Deborah Pretty and Rory Knight[1] have established that businesses that failed to manage business interruption events effectively saw a significant destruction of shareholder value. Many of the businesses Pretty and Knight studied failed altogether. Incidentally, those businesses that managed a successful recovery actually saw shareholder value rise after a disaster.

■ **Note**   Having a successful recovery can increase the value of a company. Potential investors will take that success as a sign of a well-managed firm.

Don't Waste Money on Solutions That Don't Work

You've spent a lot of money on your recovery solution, so you better be sure it works! You'd be amazed at how much money companies spend on their recovery strategies but then fail to test them.

---

[1] www.piersystem.com/external/content/document/1942/293139/1/Impacts%20 on%20share%20value%20study.pdf

In practical terms, if you haven't tested the solution and resolved the inherent issues, it won't work. In other words, you might as well have saved the money and not bothered.

Testing Is Just Good Practice

Finally, while all these things add weight to the necessity to test, testing is just good practice. Not testing is not just unprofessional—it's negligent.

Test or Exercise?

Is it a *test* or an *exercise*? People use these terms very loosely, and that includes myself! For the purposes of this book, the difference is that when testing, the principal objective is to identify faults.

By contrast, exercises set out with a more educational agenda that is focused on exposing people to their roles and responsibilities. Exercises give people and organizations a chance to practice in a safe environment. Part of this process highlights faults in processes, real issues that highlight needs for further training or awareness.

Note that in identifying faults, I'm not aiming to prove something works. I think this is a dubious practice and one that is all but impossible because you can only understand what is being tested and understand it in the context that it is being tested. In other words, you can prove that the test didn't find any faults within the scope of what was being tested, not that there were no faults. This is about the best you can do.

The inability to "prove" something works is of itself not a problem unless you start to become unnecessarily complacent. The important thing is to design tests that provide the maximum assurance that your plan will work and reveal as many possible issues as possible. It's also important that you keep this mindset so that you are alert to different test scenarios for the future and the possibility of issues that you don't know about in the present.

Types of Testing

Before we get into the different types of testing, it's important to understand that the choice of the type of testing needs to be selected with care and with a clear purpose in mind.

Some types of test are appropriate for a certain level of maturity. In other words, you might want to do technology testing before you do full-blown business tests.

Commissioning Tests

There's a logical sequence of testing that relates to the lifecycle of the solution. Commissioning is the logical first step that you undertake when you have a new solution, be it DR for a system, DR for some critical infrastructure, a workplace recovery solution, or the resilience aspect of a new services architecture.

In essence, commissioning is the testing you do before a system, service, or solution is handed over into "business as usual" so you can be as sure as possible that it will behave and perform as it was designed and meet the overall requirements.

Depending on a number of factors, you may wish to split testing into technology and business tests. This is particularly common where the service being tested is complex or new.

Technology and Business Tests

Technology testing is an opportunity to discover any issues and iron out any problems with the technology without embroiling the business unit or department in the tests. It is, if you like, "behind closed doors" testing, so that you can fix any technical, processes, procedures, and people issues before you involve the business.

Technology testing has lots of obvious benefits. First, it saves a lot of business time spent hanging around waiting for stuff to get fixed. Second, when you test, you are sending out a powerful message about the solution. Avoid testing, and if the business sees performance issue after performance issue, they will have pretty low confidence in it. Or they will be working in anger and wonder about your competence and your capability to manage this technology for them.

Once you are confident that the solution meets its recovery objectives and will work from a technical point of view, it's time to put it through its paces and make sure that it actually works.

The key to business testing is to identify all the critical operations that need to be performed and how these can be demonstrated. To bring this all together, you should work with the business to produce a test script that sets out all the tests that are to be performed and who needs to perform them.

Responsibility for producing the test would normally fall to the unit's own business continuity coordinator rather than the central business continuity management team. The central team drives the creation of the test scripts, gives direction, and supports the business coordinators. It also collects the scripts and analyzes the output.

A key area where business continuity adds value is by trying to achieve as many synergies as possible. The best way to do that is to minimize the number of people required to test all the critical processes and systems. To see what I mean, consider an example where five different departments all use the same system in exactly the same way. In this case, you wouldn't have five different people brought in to do the same test—one or two would do. Business continuity managers also add value by making sure that the test scripts reconcile with what the business has identified as critical systems and activities in their plans.

When looking for synergies and savings, you have to do it in the context of the overall objectives of testing. Part of the challenge and art of testing is balancing often-competing goals such as cutting costs and maximizing involvement to increase familiarity with the solution. The test script can help to ensure that you have balanced the objectives and make the most of your test time. And once created, the scripts ensure that business users methodically test everything.

After the commissioning tests, it's normal to reuse the scripts for test after test. However, as part of each subsequent test, you should review your test scripts to make sure they still reflect your plans and cover the critical processes and systems. It's also normal to record the actual outcomes of each test and any issues and grade the success of each operation directly onto the test script.

The analysis of the data from the test scripts forms the backbone of the test report, and, hence, all the test scripts need to be gathered before the test ends and collated to assess the overall successes and failures.

All issues that arise need to be followed up, and that follow-up process should include feeding back to the testers what was done to fix the issue and other relevant information such as why something was not an issue.

IT Service Role Swapping

With increased use of resilient architectures that straddle more than one location, there is a shift from traditional DR testing, where you bring up the contingency machine in the DR site, do a brief test, then return to the normal worksite, to switching workload to the contingency site and running production for a period of time, normally a week, then swapping back.

I've included this, called role swapping, under types of testing, although you could argue that it's not testing but just a business-as-usual process. Many organizations routinely switch their workload between sites, sometimes running for a week before switching back. Then they repeat the switches often.

Unlike other tests, there's no test script because all activities and processes are undertaken from the secondary site routinely. There's no test reporting, and any issues are not test issues to be managed by the business continuity or IT service continuity team. They are simply business-as-usual issues to be escalated as any other production issue would be.

Capacity Testing

With capacity testing, the objective is to prove that capacity meets the likely demands that will be placed on a solution in a contingency scenario. (*Contingent* because you roll over to a recovery center contingent upon a disaster or interruption in the normal place of operation.)

For most organizations these days, contingency solutions are exact matches with the production environments, so they have the same processing, storage, and network bandwidth.

In some situations, contingency may present excessive capacity challenges. For example, if a service has been down, there may be a backlog of transactions to be processed or a surge in demand once it becomes available. In addition to IT service recovery, workplace recovery may present a different set of challenges. For example, you may find that your recovery facility has to cope with a high number of people arriving at the same time that are unfamiliar with the site and don't have access. So how do you get 500 people through the door and to their desks and working in 30 minutes in the pouring rain?

Testing Scenarios

You should use scenarios as the focus of your testing approach. By this I mean you should aim to test a scenario, not the equipment. For example, rather than the aim of the test being "To ensure you can bring up the DR environment," the scenario should be something like "You have lost your head office building, which also hosts your production data center."

You are testing whether you can deal with the scenario without breaching your preagreed-to thresholds, like downtime, quality of service, delivery of critical activities, and so forth.

■ **Note**   Testing isn't about testing sites or equipment per se. Instead you are testing to make sure you can meet the standards and thresholds outlined in your plan. That might be recovering a certain function in a certain number of hours, delivering a certain quality of service, and ensuring a process remains operational, among others.

Focusing on scenarios brings some reality to the test. It forces you to examine some issues that may get swept under the carpet otherwise.

In practice, scenarios can relate to multiple tests. So if you lose the head office, you have to switch over to DR and invoke your WAR business strategy. The selection of the scenario should reflect your risks. So if your data center is on a fault line, you should test based on an earthquake first, then work your way through the other scenarios in order of risk.

It's a good idea to coordinate your testing across all locations and keep good records of the scenarios tested so you can be sure that all relevant scenarios have been tested.

Scenario Suggestions

Here are some suggestions for possible scenarios to test. You should find it easy to tailor these or come up with your own or combine them.

- Loss of production data center
- Denial of access at data center
- Power failure at production data center
- Generator failure following power loss
- Loss of one suite in a data center
- Loss of connectivity to the data center
- Loss of key office
- Loss of secondary data center
- Loss of data center that is colocated with a key office
- Denial of service attacks on your customer-facing systems
- Cyber attack or hack either from external criminals or internal employees
- Data corruption
- Contamination of your production facilities
- Supplier failure
- Blackmail
- Sabotage by a disgruntled employee

When you create your scenario, it's important to think about the timing of the test. It has a bearing on what you will actually have to do in response and by implication the range of things actually being tested.

For example, if the scenario is the data center loss and you do it during one business day, the activities are going to be very different than if you planned it to take place after the end of all batch processing and before the start of the next day. Take time to think about the limitations of your test and how in the future you can test these or otherwise mitigate any related risks.

Conduct Desktop Walkthrough Exercises

Desktop exercises should be the foundation of your overall testing strategy. Basically, it involves bringing the key people involved in the recovery together and then walking them through a scenario so you can observe how they respond and what they say they would do. Ideally, they should work from the plan, but in practice people rarely do.

Personally, I like to observe. I let things run a while then call a "timeout." During the timeout, I get the team to reflect on where they are, what they are doing, and what they should be doing. If necessary, I direct them back to their plan and challenge its validity or, if it is valid, get them to do what it says if they have deviated from it.

Desktop Walkthrough Roles

You will ideally have some support during the exercise, as it can be difficult to capture all the learning points while you are also driving the exercise forward. I like to split responsibilities with a partner, so one of us is focused on driving the scenario and the other is observing and doing the timeouts.

You need to be clear about your role, and you need to make that clear to everyone attending. Are you "in role," as the business recovery coordinator or IT lead, or are you "out of role" and directing or observing the exercise?

I do not recommend running it and observing it at the same time. So, if you need help running or observing the exercise, get it.

Desktop Walkthrough Availability

Obviously, when you do the test, not everyone will be available. If you are unfortunate enough to have to invoke your plans for real, key people won't be available. Naturally, then it makes sense for the people doing the exercise to rotate. So, for one test have the primary person in role and next time get their backup. Try to mix it up so there are not all primaries or backups but a mixture of the two.

If you can't get either the backup or primary person on the day of the test, then think about what this would mean if it were a real invocation and not just a test.

With this in mind, do you need to make sure you have cover available at all times for all key roles, like the primary business recovery coordinator and their backup? Should they never be away at the same time? If this is not practical, will you have to consider having more than one backup?

Leveraging Scenarios

It requires quite a bit of upfront effort to prepare the scenario, but once you have the scenario, it can be reused for other departments, locations, or plans. This is especially true when it comes to business continuity plans. Here you should use the same scenario with all plans each year so you build a comprehensive picture of your ability to deal with each scenario and offer assurances to management and other stakeholders that you are able to deal with key scenarios at an enterprise level.

It's a good idea to build a library of scenarios so they can be reused with ease. It's also worth networking with peers in your industry and other people doing BCM generally, as you'll probably find they are indeed proud to share their scenarios with you.

Tip Network with other business continuity and disaster recovery planners in other companies. You can learn a lot from one another about how to deal with specific scenarios.

Level of Scenario Detail

When testing, if you're not familiar with the plan, you're in trouble. You will need to be very familiar with it so you can give appropriate direction during the exercise, detect when the team is off plan, and pick up areas that need improvement or lack clarity.

The level of detail you put into the scenario depends on your personal style, the culture, and expectations. In my experience, a simple scenario that is well structured but lacks visual aids and other bells and whistles works well and requires about 10% of the effort to prepare than a technology-rich exercise.

The culture and expectations as well as your ability should determine the nature of the exercise. Remember, it's not what you want or enjoy that counts—it's what's needed and what the client expects to see!

I remember an exercise where a colleague spent weeks of his personal time adding video feeds, CNN, and BBC news items, mocked up images, and real interaction with the emergency services to create a realistic scenario. It looked great, and my colleague and I loved delivering it, but the risk director, who was a "no-frills" type, was totally unimpressed and wondered how we'd found so much time to do all the bells and whistles. All that she felt was needed was a simple script. She was the customer, so that's what we should have given her, or we should have persuaded her that she needed more before we started building the scenario.

You live and learn, and making these mistakes is school-boy stuff, but we all do it. Believe me, it's better that someone tells you in advance that your planned approach is no good than they think that the final result is no good!

Action Plan

Review the following questions and consider if you need to follow the recommendations:

1. If you tested services and solutions, how confident are you that these would really work if you needed to recover?

2. Have you identified the correct types of testing to do, and do they evolve appropriately (i.e., desktop walkthroughs, technology tests, business tests, and capacity tests)?

3. Have you looked at your choice of scenarios, types of testing, and test scripts to make sure you are balancing all the objectives while balancing costs and disruption?

4. Have you tested using the most likely scenarios? Are these scenarios changed each test cycle (i.e., every year)? Would it be prudent to adopt a different scenario for your next test?

5. Do you perform regular desktop exercises? If not, review the section "Conduct Desktop Walkthrough Exercise."

IT Disaster Recovery Testing

Things You Need to Know

Here are the keys to successful IT disaster recovery tests:

- Apply basic project management tools to DR tests
- Assign roles and responsibility
- Use a scenario-based approach
- Plan well
- Engage management
- Provide the right resources
- Test regularly
- Manage risk
- Report results quickly

The majority of this chapter expands on these aspects of successful DR testing.

Apply Basic Project Management Tools to Disaster Recovery Tests

Although IT DR testing should be part of your business-as-usual activities, each test is a project in its own right. Each test has:

- A defined starting point
- Objectives
- Deliverables
- Quality standards
- Work plan or schedule
- Resources
- Risks and issues
- A defined end point

Furthermore, each test is a unique piece of work. In short, you should approach testing with all the rigor that is normal for your organization when undertaking a project of this scale.

How much project management you provide hinges on what's appropriate. If the test involves one person and only takes a few hours to prepare, then clearly you don't need formal project management. However, what if it involves months of preparation, high risks, or the coordination of many teams? Then project management is not just useful but should be a mandatory requirement.

Again, depending on the scale of the test, you might want to secure the services of an experienced and professional project manager. If it's manageable or you have dedicated specialist to manage DR tests, you can skip the project manager, but you should still expect the people leading the work to apply basic project management methods and tools to the work in accordance with your organization's standards.

■ **Note** Key things that you'll need to focus on before and during tests are securing the right resources, managing risks and issues, prebooking test slots, communicating progress and expectations, and managing stakeholders.

Assign Disaster Recovery Testing Roles and Responsibilities

Roles and responsibilities can be split among:

- Preparatory work
- Testing phase: the actual DR test
- Observation: observing the test
- Issue fix: fixing issues

Let's look at each of these in greater depth.

Preparatory Roles and Responsibilities

From my experience, about 80% of the work that goes into a test is preparing for the test. Key activities include planning the test, preparing test scripts for both technologists and end users, identifying issues that will prevent a successful test, fixing issues, training, writing instructions and supporting documentation, and component testing.

The majority of this work is undertaken by IT technical staff. However, depending on the complexity of the test, it can involve dozens of different specialists. The following key disciplines are likely to be involved:

- Network engineers
- Platform or operating systems specialists
- Applications support
- Middleware support
- Database administrators
- Data center operations
- Storage specialists
- Information security specialists
- IT service continuity
- Change or incident management

Two things are critical to the success of the overall test and being ready for the testing phase in particular. These two things are the coordination of all the people and ensuring all the actions are captured and resolved in good time.

Testing Roles and Responsibilities

During the testing phase, there are always people who need to perform critical tasks in a particular sequence. This requires both planning and efficient organization to ensure that the activity moves smoothly between discrete disciplines.

Critical to the success of the test is making sure that everyone understands their responsibilities and that everyone communicates when they have completed their tasks to those who are waiting to follow them and anyone who is keeping track of progress against the recovery plan.

This cascade is critical when recovering, as you need to keep things moving, as well as when testing and you want to capture accurate timings.

Observation Roles and Responsibilities

When testing you need to establish:

- Whether the people did exactly what the plan says they should have done. If not, then either their behavior needs to change or the plans need to change to reflect the correct actions.

- How long it really takes to recover the IT systems and how much, if any, data were lost.

- What issues arose, and, if they were fixed, exactly how this was achieved.

I have to confess that in my days as a systems programmer, I rarely followed any plans. Typically, like most of your technical staff, I knew how to do things, so I just got on with it.

That was fine, as long as I was available or, in your case, the techy who already knows what to do is available. But will someone who knows exactly what to do when disaster strikes be available? If the expert is not available and the instructions aren't clear in the plans, you're in trouble.

Also, another issue is that if your techies just wing your tests and don't systematically work through the instructions, you'll learn nothing about the validity of the plans, which after all is a key element that is really being tested and learned.

While I'm in confession mode, the truth is that while winging it I often fail to take the time to make sure the steps I actually performed and the things I fixed to make it work were included in the plans.

To be frank, I was too busy trying to get things to work to think about what I was doing and keep a record. It's likely that the vast majority of the people who will be doing your recovery will operate in a similar fashion.

One of your planning assumptions should therefore always be that the "expert" is unavailable. Your plans must be written so that a competent generalist could perform the recovery.

■ **Tip**   Assume at all times that in a real disaster, the resident expert will not be available. That means there should be clear directions at every step that an IT generalist can perform to recover systems.

To make sure you improve the plans so they reflect the real recovery steps at an appropriate level of detail and that all issues and timings are kept, you need to make someone responsible for monitoring the technical recovery staff to ensure they are doing exactly what the plans says. They must also be correcting any errors in their process and updating the plans to reflect these changes.

You must select people for these sorts of observational roles with care. They need to have an eye for detail, great people skills, and a thick skin. They need to be able to build rapport with the people performing and coordinating the recovery activities without getting in their hair. They need to deal with people who will probably be very rude and perhaps even aggressive. Trust me—few people are more rude and unpleasant than a techy who is being observed and forced to conform to a rigorous approach that encroaches on their freedom.

At these times, your observers need resolve and a focus on the objective. They need to demonstrate empathy and understanding for people who are probably stressed, lacking social skills, thinking that the observer is keeping them from doing their job, and are unable to "get" why someone wants to know what the issues are.

To make observation as smooth as possible, you need:

- A simple command-and-control structure that includes the feedback of progress against key milestones (timings) and issues.

- Clearly defined responsibilities for all those who are performing recovery actions. These responsibilities should include recording progress, issues, and deviations from the documented recovery steps.

- To make sure that everyone understands why you are testing (i.e., "We are testing principally to find issues then fix and document them.").

Two things that can make your life much easier are test scripts and test software, as discussed in the following sections.

Test Scripts

Recovery test scripts are a simple tool to ensure that not only the correct recovery steps get tested but also that any issues and timings are captured so the recovery process can be improved and the overall recovery time objectives can be demonstrated. In its simplest form, they simply set out all the recovery steps with suitable space for comments and timings. That way, whoever does the recovery can work from the script and keep a record of issues and timings in one place.

It's normal to have separate scripts for the technical staff doing the recovery and any business users doing user testing.

Technical Recovery Test Scripts

The technical recovery script is normally a direct extract of the recovery procedures that needs to be followed to complete the recovery process. The key aims in the technical phase of recovery testing are, first, to ensure that the recovery process is effective and adequately detailed for someone of limited direct knowledge of the system to complete the recovery. The second aim is to gather the timings so you will know if it is possible to meet the businesses recovery time objective.

Business Test Scripts

The business test script sets out all the critical business activities. It's worth working through the script with the business contact to make sure it reflects all the critical activities they do and make sure that all the systems, files, and tools are covered. Be specific and, as far as possible, follow the flow of business activities. That way, if something is booked on one system, amended on another, and printed on a third system, you can ensure the data are consistent among all and that the actual business flow works.

The scope of the test script will reflect the scope of the test. If you are only testing the recovery of a single server or service it might not be meaningful or possible to test flow.

When designing your testing, think about the impact of what you're doing and any potential risks. Be careful if data are being entered on to live databases or can flow from the system being tested to a downstream live system.

There's no excuse for not having scripts. Not only can they vastly improve the effectiveness of your tests, but making them auditable can help to significantly reduce the risks associated with testing.

Test Software

The ideal situation in testing is to use automated software, such as Test Director, which includes your scripts, captures timings and issues, and, at the end, produces instant reporting.

Although preparing scripts is quite easy and inexpensive, software, on the other hand, is expensive and more of a strategic decision for your organization. But check around in the IT department; someone may already be using Test Director or something similar.

Issue Fix for Disaster Recovery Tests

There's little point in doing any tests if you're not going to address any issues that emerge while testing.

Have patience when discovering new and unknown issues that threaten the viability of your recovery capability. However, don't be tolerant when it comes to discovering an issue that still exists from an earlier test.

I recommend that for any issue:

- You identify the person or people who can fix it.
- That the senior managers who control resources are made accountable for a problem's timely resolution.
- Resources are allocated, work planned, and timescales agreed upon to fix the issue.
- You monitor the progress of those fixing the issue, ideally tracking progress against milestones.
- You escalate any failure to progress an issue immediately.

In terms of roles and responsibilities, I'd also recommend that the BCM manager tracks all issues centrally and regularly reviews progress, and that those performing the fix are made aware of the timelines and agree-upon milestones, if that is appropriate. Finally, accountable managers must actually be held accountable for ensuring that reasonable progress is made.

Use Scenario-Based Disaster Recovery Testing

Scenario-based testing is important. The driver here is to ensure that what you're testing is consistent with the organization's most likely and highest-impact scenarios. Testing should also contribute to an enterprise-wide understanding of the exposure to the key scenarios. In addition, testing should be progressive; each subsequent test provides greater confidence in the viability of the recovery solution and reduces the overall risk.

I always recommend that if you are doing several DR tests across the organization, you should align the tests to the same scenario. For example, you would dictate that every DR test in a given year should use "loss of power, followed by backup power supply failure" as the scenario.

The exception to when you might not want to use the current enterprise test scenario is in the case of a one-off commissioning test. This is the testing that you do as part of the acceptance process when creating a new DR solution.

For commissioning, I'd use the most likely scenario and generally focus on technical recovery. Then, once DR is live and it's time to do the next business-as-usual test, fall in with the enterprise scenario for that year.

As I said earlier, our job is to be relentless in the search for issues that might prevent a successful recovery. If you don't find any errors when you test, change the test next time and use a different scenario. Never assume that just because the past test found no issues there are none.

Note   Just because a test went smoothly doesn't mean your process doesn't have hidden problems. To root them out, try a different scenario next time.

Most don't consider scenarios when testing. Consequently, their tests are limited and don't reveal previously unknown issues. Most tests, by default, operate with the scenario element that the event has happened after an orderly closedown and all batches have been completed. This is because this is when most tests are done. The problem is that most outages happen in the middle of a production day and are disorderly. Consequently, when people deploy their contingency solution for real, a lot of issues emerge that either delay recovery or, all too often, render its use more problematic than just having an extended outage. This is insane, and you might as well save your money and not have any DR.

Plan DR Tests Well

Successful testing is a product of the effort that goes into preparing for the test. Coordinating all the resources, resolving all the issues, and making sure that everything happens on time require sound planning.

Engage Management in the Disaster Recovery Test

Projects often fail because there's a lack of resources and a lack of focus. Often this is because the accountability for the project isn't clear. Chances are you may feel accountable for the success of what you're doing, but in practice you may not have the ultimate power to ensure that things are resourced and issues get escalated. So the sense of accountability will only lead to stress and frustration.

Bottom line is that you're more likely to be "responsible" for doing things rather than being "accountable" for making sure they get done, or indeed responsible if they fail!

Accountability must be clearly defined and allocated. The person accountable must be in a position to secure resources and be able to support those who have responsibility for doing the necessary work.

So, make sure that accountability is defined and allocated to a suitable individual. If at all possible, avoid having the accountability sitting with a body of people, because you'll find it harder to get the support you need or secure quick responses to key questions and requests. Committees rarely feel the same sense of "skin in the game" as an individual, and they generally can't respond quickly because there is a built-in lag time that delays decisions until the next planned meeting or until you can otherwise secure consensus and approval.

Having identified the accountability and allocated it, make sure that the accountable person is suitably briefed on their accountability, the related work that's planned, and all the key issues that affect them.

Make sure those accountable receive regular reporting. Don't bury them in data, but instead report by exception. That means you report when things don't go according to plan. Tell them about progress against milestones, issues, and how they are being resolved, or not.

In practice, you tell them what reporting you'll be giving them. If they really need something different, they will tell you. In my experience, if you ask people what they want, you'll end up having to cut your data 10 different ways to accommodate all the different expectations from the different stakeholders.

Note   Accountability is different from responsibility. The accountable party typically can dispense resources, settle some disputes, provide support, and so forth. Responsibility is about ensuring specific tasks are done according to plan. The accountable person, in short, makes sure the responsible person can get the required job done.

Disaster Recovery Test Kickoff Meetings

Once you have identified the principal stakeholders in the DR test, get them together and agree to:

- Test objectives: What do you aim to achieve?

- Test scope: What are you going to test and what are you not going to test? Be specific at the outset about what's not going to be tested; it makes for clarity later and sets clear expectations.

- Approach: How are you going to approach the test? For example, will you operate as a split site with live users working both in production as normal and some contingency workers working from DR?

- Test scenario: What scenario is going to be used for planning the test?

- Metrics: How will you measure success and progress?

- Roles and responsibilities: who will do what?

- Reporting and regular meetings: How will you report progress and issues, and what meetings should there be?

I'd strongly urge you not to use this meeting to figure out all these things. Instead, go into the meeting with a set of recommendations, backed with supporting arguments. Use the meeting to challenge them and, where possible, arrive at improvements or alternatives.

The reason I make this suggestion is that in my experience, teams are very bad at brainstorming these types of ideas; they tend toward procrastination and complacence. Teams often work best when given something specific to evaluate and improve. It brings focus and momentum.

I'd also recommend that when you start the meeting, you should already be confident that what you are suggesting is going to be broadly acceptable and you will have enough support in the room.

After the meeting you should formalize what conclusions were reached with regard to the above points by recording them in project documents, such as "terms of reference" or something similar. Then make sure that all stakeholders and senior management review and approve them.

Try to avoid the comprehensive approach to "kickoff" meetings where project managers invite everyone and their dog in the hopes of covering everything.

Be focused, only invite people who need to be there and who can make a meaningful contribution.

Hold Regular Disaster Recovery Test Meetings

Once the DR test project is under way, it's essential that you regularly reconvene the key people to review progress and identify risks and issues.

Make sure these meetings are brief. Always prepare an agenda and record any issues in the minutes. Also, add the details of any salient discussion to the minutes, but keep them brief and focus on conclusions and the key supporting rationale. Capture actions and issues and make sure they get reviewed each time you meet.

Provide the Right Resources

Human resources are always an issue in business, and, in particular, getting the right ones at the right time.

DR testing is a little unusual in that for the actual test phase, you may want to have a less-experienced resource, one that's not actually familiar with the product or package so that you can test whether the plan is fit for the purpose.

When using inexperienced people, you should make sure they receive adequate support. You don't want them to fail. What you want to do is flush out any issue either with the plan or the recovery strategy and, wherever possible, fix these things as you go along.

For the rest of the test, you'll be constrained by the same issues as any business activity. You want the right people available when you need them. This comes back to good planning, solid stakeholder management, and clear management accountability, which can be leveraged to secure the resources.

Keep a close eye on the resources that get allocated. It's pretty common to get offered some inappropriate people and for their team managers to just leave them to sink or swim.

The key is to monitor progress against milestones. Look for tangible signs of progress. Don't be satisfied with "it's 80% done" feedback. Get answers, specifically, to questions like: "What have you done?" "What remains to be done?, "What issues do you have?", and "What issues or barriers do you foresee?"

If you have doubts about the resources you have been given and they are not getting adequate support, escalate it as soon as possible.

Test Regularly

For testing to be effective, it must be conducted regularly. The exact frequency is a balance between cost and risk.

In practice, it's hard to test most large systems more than once a year. However, if you leave it for much more than a year, the chance of problems emerging increases significantly.

In some rare cases, you may have an obligation to test more than once a year. For example, it may be a contractual requirement to test two times a year.

I recommend making testing a key element of your business continuity policy. I'd also recommend that you set out some standards, such as critical systems must be tested annually; noncritical systems must be tested at least once every two years.

Tip Make testing a key element of your business continuity policy. Specify, in particular, the frequency you'll test various critical systems.

Manage Test Risk

You need to remember that testing in and of itself can be a risky business. You are moving live data and sometimes you will also be running live systems as part of your test.

DR testing comes with a number of risks. These include:

- Corruption of live data
- Breach of data-protection rules
- Breach of security
- Outage of production service
- Failure to return to normal operations after the test
- Impairment to production services—where the test may take resources away from production
- Taking technical resources away from production, support, and critical development work

You should always start with a high-level risk assessment for the test, with particular focus on impact on production, operational issues, and security issues.

You need to use this insight when selecting your scenario and designing your test so that the risks can be minimized and mitigated. Much of the preparation work will be directed toward setting things up to minimize or avoid risks.

You should arrive at a point where the risks of doing the test are far less than not doing it. If you don't get to this point, you have to go back to the drawing board!

Finally, remember that the risk isn't yours, and it's almost certainly not an IT risk, although IT may think it is. Whose risk is it? It's a business risk. So, it's critical that the risk is formally documented and an appropriate risk owner identified and made aware. That person should approve the proposed testing.

Report Results Quickly

In testing, you must capture the key learnings, create a set of actions, and make them public. If you don't, the test is not worth your time.

The audience for the reports can be grouped as follows:

- Management: Show that everything is okay and, where there are issues, you have planned suitable work to fix them.

- Technical staff: Let them know exactly what the issues are, what's been agreed upon, and who is doing it.

- Auditors. Let them see that appropriate controls are in place, that you have identified potential breaches, and that you are managing them professionally. They will also want to see evidence that the tests are consistent with best practice and your internal policies.

I find it a good practice to have two test reports: a flash report and a full report.

Flash Report

The purpose of the flash report is to get the key test results out quickly. It covers success or failure and some basic metrics. It doesn't include rationale, analysis, or recommendations.

It's ideally issued on the final day of the test, or, at the very least, within a few working days of the test finishing.

The flash report summarizes each element of the test and sets out whether it was a success or failure. Keep it simple, and use traffic lights or something similar so people can look at it and instantly get a feel of how the test went.

Full Report

The full report is comprehensive and provides evidence and relevant rationale to support the findings. However, for the benefit of the majority of its readers, the full report should also have a management summary that presents the key findings and supporting rationale in one or two pages.

Issue the full report within a month of the test. The exact timing depends on completion of the posttest meetings and any related analysis.

The posttest meeting is the forum where all the issues from the test should be discussed and actions and owners agreed upon. The full report sets out all the issues, actions, timescales, and recommendations. It normally takes 2 weeks to pull together for a large test, so don't overpromise. Allow additional time if you have to get it past a number of stakeholders who have to agree on the findings before it is issued!

Closing a Disaster Recovery Test

You might think that the production of the final report signifies the end of the test as a project. However, there's a need to make a formal distinction between the test as a project and ongoing business-as-usual activities.

There's a danger that your tests could lack a clear end point with issues being managed for months or years after the actual tests. It's important to draw an end to the project and transition any lingering issues into business as usual.

I'd strongly recommend that when the final test report is published, you would have already transitioned everything related to the test into business as usual. The key thing to do is to ensure that all actions are owned and they continue to be tracked but not part of the project. In addition to outstanding issues, you need to ensure that everything that has been learned as part of the test is being used to its fullest.

Finally, you have to move the people who have been working on the project back to their normal roles or other projects, and in doing this, it's very important that you provide them and their managers with feedback on their performance, contribution, and behaviors. This final people point is often overlooked, and people fail to capitalize on the development opportunity or recognition for their efforts.

Action Plan

Review the following questions and consider if you need to follow the recommendations:

1. If you tested services and solutions, how confident are you that they would really work if you needed to recover?

2. Have you tested using the most likely scenarios? Are these scenarios changed each test cycle, perhaps every year? Would it be prudent to adopt a different scenario for your next test?

3. Do you perform regular desktop exercises? If not, review the desktop walkthrough exercises in Chapter 11

4. Are all the issues documented and owned and do they have a viable action plan? Do you track your actions to make sure that progress is being made? Do you have a process to escalate issues? If not, then look at how you can embed appropriate action tracking into your processes.

5. Are your tests adequately resourced with suitably skilled people, and do you give everyone who could be involved (alternates as well as primary responders) the chance to gain experience?

6. Do you test frequently enough?

7. Are you identifying and managing the risks associated with testing?

8. Are test reports produced quickly, and do they provide the stakeholders with the information they need?

9. Are your tests scripted so they cover the key operations that are required in recovery and the tests can be repeated?

10. Are users fully involved with the testing?

11. At the time you publish the final test report, do all the outstanding risks and issues have owners and action plans and are they set up so that they will be managed to completion after the test is closed?

Business Recovery Testing

Things You Need to Know About Work Area Recovery Testing

The elements that make up successful WAR (work area recovery) tests are the same as those that make up successful IT DR tests:

- Apply basic project management tools to DR tests
- Assign roles and responsibility
- Use a scenario-based approach
- Plan well
- Engage management
- Provide the right resources
- Test regularly
- Manage risk
- Report results quickly

The majority of this chapter expands on these aspects of successful business continuity testing.

Apply Basic Project Management Tools to Work Area Recovery Tests

WAR, just like DR testing, should be part of your business-as-usual activity. Each test is a project in its own right as every test has:

- A defined starting point
- Objectives
- Deliverables
- Quality standards
- Work plan or schedule
- Resources
- Risks and issues
- A defined end point

Each test is a unique piece of work, and you should approach WAR testing with the rigor that is appropriate in your organization when undertaking a project of a similar scale.

The key to how much project management hinges on what's appropriate. If the test involves one person and takes a few hours to prepare and do it, then clearly it doesn't warrant being wrapped in project management.

If, however, it involves some or all of months of preparation, significant risks, and the coordination of many people, clearly project management isn't just useful, but should be considered a mandatory requirement.

Again, depending on the scale of the test, you might want to secure the services of a project manager. If it's manageable or you have dedicated specialists who normally manage WAR tests, you can skip the project manager. However the test is managed, you must expect the people leading the work to apply basic project management and to do the work in accordance with your organization's standards.

The key things you'll need to review are securing the right resources, managing risks and issues, prebooking test slots, communicating progress and expectations, and managing stakeholders.

Assign Work Area Recovery Testing Roles and Responsibilities

Roles and responsibilities can be split among:

- Preparatory work
- Testing phase: the actual WAR test
- Observation: observing the test
- Issue fix: fixing issues

Let's look at each of these in greater depth.

Work Area Recovery Preparatory Roles and Responsibilities

Just like DR, about 80% of the work that makes up a test involves preparing for the test. Key activities include planning the test, repairing test scripts for both technologists and end users, identifying issues that will prevent a successful test, fixing issues, training, writing instructions and the supporting document, and component testing.

The majority of this work is undertaken by IT technical staff. However, just like DR, depending on the complexity of the test, it can involve dozens of different specialists. However, as a general rule the following key disciplines will need to be involved:

- Networks
- Desktop support
- Applications support
- Change or incident management
- Facilities or security

Critical to the success of the overall test and ensuring you are ready for the testing is the coordination of all these people and ensuring all the actions are captured and resolved in a timely manner.

Testing Roles and Responsibilities

As with any test, there are a number of people who need to perform critical tasks in the correct sequence. You'll need to plan in depth and make sure your organization is running smoothly to ensure the different disciplines and people mesh.

Everyone must understand their responsibilities, and everyone must communicate when they have completed their tasks to those who are waiting to follow them, as well as anyone keeping track of progress against the recovery plan.

This sequence is critical when recovering. You need to keep things moving and capture accurate timings.

Observation Roles and Responsibilities for Work Area Recovery Tests

When testing you need to establish that:

- People have actually done what the plan says. If not, then either their behavior needs to change or the plans need to change.

- How long it takes to recover the business and how much information is lost, if any.

- Any issues that came up were fixed and how.

As always, assume that "experts" are unavailable in the midst of a disaster; therefore, write plans so a competent generalist could perform the recovery.

Technicians are also notoriously poor at keeping records of what they do, what doesn't work, or how long things actually take. To be frank, they're busy people, and they're trying to get things to work, so you shouldn't be surprised if they seem too busy thinking about what they're doing to keep a record.

To make sure that we improve the plans so they reflect the real recovery steps and that these steps are recorded at an appropriate level of detail, make someone responsible for keeping records and monitoring what actually happens. Having an independent observer will enable you to improve your plans and capture all issues and timings.

Again, just as for IT DR testing, select people who will not just observe and report on testing activity; they must do it all with finesse, as they need to have an eye for detail, great people skills, and thick skin.

Observers need to demonstrate resolve and maintain a focus on the objective. They need to demonstrate empathy and understanding of people who may be stressed and probably think that the observer's questions and presence are keeping them from doing their job.

To make observation as smooth as possible, you need:

- A simple command-and-control structure, which includes feedback of progress against key milestones (timings) and issues.
- Clearly defined responsibilities for all those who are performing recovery actions, which includes recording progress, issues, and deviations from the documented recovery steps.

Recovery scripts and test software can make your life much easier.

Recovery Test Scripts

Just as for IT DR, recovery test scripts used for your WAR solution set out all the recovery steps with suitable space for comments and timings. That way, the technicians doing the recovery can work from the script and keep a record of issues and timings in one place.

Business Test Script

It's normal to have separate scripts for the technical staff doing the recovery and any business users who will be testing at the recovery site.

The business test script sets out all the critical business activities. I'd recommend that you always walk through the business test script with business management to make sure that all the critical activities and systems used are covered. When preparing the script, be specific and as far as possible follow the flow of business activities to make sure the data are consistent between it and the actual business flow works.

Think too of the risks when designing your testing. Remember that data being entered onto live databases can flow from the system being tested to a downstream live system if you're not careful. I generally get people to go to the recovery site and just work as normal but get them to review the test script at the start of the day and sign it all off at the end.

There's no excuse for not having auditable scripts. They improve your tests and reduce the risks associated with testing.

Tip It's worth walking the floor to see where people are against their test scripts. Often what you'll find is that they are either sitting on issues or haven't done anything yet. If you're not careful, you'll find that people will come in and do their work and leave without completing the test script.

Test Software

The ideal situation is to use automated test software, which includes your scripts, captures timings and issues, and produces instant reporting. Test Director is a good product; see if your IT department has a copy.

Issue Fix for Work Area Recovery Tests

Address any issues that emerge during the test.

Be positive when it comes to discovering new and unknown issues that undermine the recovery capability. Don't get upset, because it's the search for issues that is the reason for testing—you want to find them and then fix them!

Having said that, don't be tolerant when it comes to discovering an issue that still exists from an earlier test. If this happens, look at this realistically and make sure that people don't commit this crime twice!

For any issue I recommend that:

- You identify the person or people who can fix it.

- The senior managers who control resources are made accountable for a problem's timely resolution.

- Resources are allocated, work planned, and timescales agreed upon to fix the issue.

- You monitor the progress of those fixing the issue, ideally tracking progress against milestones.

- You escalate any failure to progress an issue immediately.

In terms of roles and responsibilities, I'd recommend that:

- The BCM manager tracks all issues centrally and regularly reviews progress resolving the issue.

- Those performing the fix are made aware of the milestones, timelines, and the visibility of the issue.

- The accountable managers are held accountable for reasonable progress.

Use Scenario-Based Testing for Work Area Recovery

Remember, you want to test in a way consistent with the types of scenarios that are most likely to come about. These will in turn be the most educational and useful in case the real thing happens. Finally, they will give you greater confidence in your recovery solution.

If you are doing several WAR tests across the organization, align them all to test the same scenario. Every WAR test in a given year could use, for example, denial of access as the scenario.

Note The exception to running the same scenario in all areas would be the commissioning test that you do as part of the acceptance process when creating a new WAR solution. For commissioning, I'd recommend using the most likely scenario; then for the subsequent business-as-usual test, I'd align with the enterprise scenario for that year.

As mentioned previously, our job is to be relentless in the search for issues that might prevent a successful recovery. If you don't find any errors when you test, change the test next time and use a different scenario. Never assume because the test finds no issues there are none.

Plan Well for WAR Tests

Successful testing is largely a product of the effort that goes into preparing for the test. Coordinating all the resources, resolving all the issues, and making sure that everything happens on time require rigorous planning.

Engage Management in Work Area Recovery Tests

Projects often fail because there's a lack of resources and focus. Often this is because there's a lack of effective accountability. You must find ways to engage accountable managers in the WAR tests. After all, if you feel accountable for the success of what you're doing but don't have the power to ensure you have the resources you need, you will experience stress and anxiety, which are not consistent with success.

Accountability must be clearly defined and allocated. The accountable person must be in a position to secure resources and support, no matter who has responsibility for specific actions.

Note Avoid accountability resting with a body of people. You'll find it hard going to get support. Committees rarely feel the same sense of responsibility as an individual, and it can be very hard to get the required approval when there is no scheduled meeting.

Having identified and allocated the accountability, make sure that the account-able person is suitable and receives regular exception reporting. Don't bury that person in data; detail those things that need attention and are immediately visible. Report on progress against milestones, issues, and how these are being resolved, or not.

In practice, tell them what reporting you'll be giving them. If they really need something different, they will tell you.

Engage Users in Work Area Recovery Testing

Getting the business engaged in WAR testing is critical for two reasons:

- It helps to add rigor to the testing. After all, only the business users can tell you if their systems and desktops work okay.

- It familiarizes the business users with the recovery strategy, the working environment at the WAR site, and the compromises that are part of working in a WAR situation.

Integrating Work Area Recovery and IT Disaster Recovery

The degree of integration with your data center DR hinges on whether your data center is colocated or very likely to be affected by a local event. For example, if the data center is on the same flood plain, supplied by the same utilities, the same disaster will affect both areas.

If the data center is colocated with business units that require recovery, it's likely that your WAR tests will be integrated with your DR. You will test both together, and users at the WAR site will access systems from the DR data center, not production services.

If that's the case, then you should also think about the possibility of a denial-of-access test that measures the viability of accessing the production services from WAR.

If your data center isn't colocated, you probably won't normally test accessing the services in WAR from the DR location. In other words, when users come in to test at the WAR site, they will log on to the normal production environment because it's a reasonable assumption that it should be unaffected by a scenario that leads to the WAR invocation.

In this case it is also worth occasionally testing access to services from the DR site. After all, the odds of losing the data center when you're already in WAR are exactly the same as on any normal day.

So, make this a scenario for one of your tests and routinely prove network connectivity every time you test. It should be possible for your network people to do, and it demonstrates that people in the WAR site can in theory connect to systems that might be running at the DR site.

Never make assumptions about things such as being able to connect between sites. You'd be surprised to know the amount of times that I've discovered there is in fact no network connection between the necessary sites. This is not an issue you can resolve that day, as network providers routinely take months to provide a connection.

Work Area Recovery Kickoff Meetings

Once you have identified the principal stakeholders in the WAR test, get them together and agree upon:

- Test objectives: What do you aim to achieve?

- Test scope: What are you going to test and what are you not going to test? Be specific at the outset about what's not going to be tested; it makes for clarity latter and sets clear expectations.

- Approach: How are you going to approach the test? For example, will you operate as a split site with live users working both in production as normal and some contingency workers working from DR?

- Test scenario: What scenario is going to be used for planning the test?

- Metrics: How will you measure success and progress?

- Roles and responsibilities: Who will do what?

- Reporting and regular meetings: How will you report progress and issues, and what meetings should there be?

Don't expect this meeting to do your job for you! Rather, go into the meeting with a set of recommendations, backed with supporting arguments. Use the meeting to get input, challenge what you're proposing, get people to buy into the test approach, and, if possible, arrive at improvements to your suggestions or more viable alternatives.

Teams work best when given clear boundaries, time limits, and something to critique and improve. It brings focus and momentum.

After the meeting you should formalize these points by recording them in a project document (e.g., a project charter, terms of reference, etc.) that all stakeholders and senior management must review and approve.

Invite only those who need to be there and can make a meaningful contribution.

Hold Regular Work Area Recovery Meetings

Once the WAR test project is under way, it's essential that you regularly reconvene the key people so you can jointly review progress and identify risks and issues.

Make sure these meetings are brief. Always prepare an agenda and record any issues in the minutes. Also, add the details of any salient discussion to the minutes, but keep these brief and focus on conclusions and the key supporting rationale. Capture actions and issues and make sure they get reviewed each time you meet.

Provide the Right Resources

Getting the right human resources at the right time is always an issue in business.

WAR testing, like DR, is unusual in that for testing purposes you may want to have a less-experienced person, one who is not actually familiar with the process they will have to follow. Using people who don't already know what they will have to do forces technically minded people to use the plan, and, in doing so, it allows you to test that the plan is fit for purpose.

Make sure everyone has support; you don't want them to fail because they lack basic skills. You want to flush out issues with the plan or recovery strategy and wherever possible fix these things as you go along. In particular, if you find an issue you want to fix, do it as quickly as possible so that the test can continue to its end.

As ever, monitor progress against milestones and look for tangible signs of progress. Don't be satisfied with the people telling you things like "It's 80% done." Find out specifically what's been done, what needs to be done, and what challenges they faced.

Test Regularly

Conduct testing regularly. How often? That's a balance between cost and risk.

In practice, it's hard to persuade business units to take time out of their planners to test more than once a year. However, if you leave it for much more than a year, the chance of problems emerging increases significantly.

If your WAR is provided by a third party, there will almost certainly be restrictions on when you can test and how often. Most mature organizations book their test slots more than a year in advance.

In practice, this means that slots are not generally available at short notice.

Most contracts restrict you to a single test a year, so you will have to make the most of this testing time. It's thus important that you think about future constraints like this when you are preparing the contract with the supplier. If it will take you 5 days to recover and test your business, then 3 days a year isn't enough!

Like DR, I'd recommend making WAR testing a key element of your policy and set out some standards. A simple example might be something like critical systems must be tested annually, noncritical at least once every 2 years.

Manage Test Risks

You need to remember that testing at your recovery site in itself can be a risky business. You're moving live data and sometimes running live systems as part of your test.

This comes with a number of risks:

- Corruption of live data
- Breach of data protection rules
- Breach of security
- Outage of production service
- Failure to return to normal operations after the test
- Degradation of production services (e.g., where the test may take resources away from production)
- Taking technical resources away from production, support and critical development work

You need to do a high-level risk assessment for the test, with particular focus on production, operational, and security issues. Use this insight when selecting your scenario and designing your test, so that the risks can be minimized and mitigated.

Note   Much of the preparation work should be directed toward setting things up to minimize or avoid risks. You should arrive at a point where the risks of doing the test are far less than not doing them. If you don't get to this point, you have to go back to the drawing board!

Document the risk formally and identify an appropriate risk owner. Make sure that person is aware of the risk and approves the proposed testing.

Report Results Quickly

It's of no value to test if you don't capture the key lessons, create a set of actions, and make them public.

There are three audiences for testing reports:

- Management, who will want assurance that everything is okay and that where there are issues there is a suitable work planned to fix them.

- Technical staff, who will need to know exactly what the issues are, what's been agreed upon, and who is doing it.

- Auditors, who will want to see that appropriate controls are in place and that breaches are identified and professionally managed.

Just as with DR, I find it a good practice to have two test reports: flash reports and full reports.

Flash Report

Use the flash report to get the results published quickly. Assess success or failure and provide some basic metrics. Don't include rationale, analysis, or recommendations.

Issue it, ideally, on the final day of the test or, at the very least, within a few working days of the test finishing.

The flash report summarizes each element of the test and states whether the test was a success or failure.

Full Report

The full report is comprehensive and provides the evidence to support the findings and any appropriate rationale. It should also have a management summary that presents the key findings and supporting rationale.

Issue the full report within a month of the test. Make sure it states all the issues, actions, timescales, and recommendations. It normally takes 2 weeks to pull all of this together for a large test, so don't overpromise, especially if you have to get it past a number of stakeholders first.

Closing a Work Area Recovery Test

The final report doesn't signify the end of the test as a project. You must make a formal distinction between the WAR test project and ongoing business-as-usual activities.

But it's important to draw an end to the project and transition any lingering issues into business as usual.

I'd strongly recommend that when the final report is released, you transition everything related to the test into business as usual. The key thing to do is to make sure that all actions are owned and they continue to be tracked but not as part of the project. In addition to outstanding issues, make sure that everything that has been learned as part of the test is being used to its full.

Finally, you have to move the people who have been working on the project back to their normal role or other projects, and in doing this it's very important that you provide them and their managers with feedback on their performance, contribution, and behaviors. This final people point is often overlooked, and people fail to capitalize on the development opportunity or get recognition for their efforts.

Action Plan

Review the following questions and consider if you need to follow the recommendations:

1. If you tested services and solutions, how confident are you that these would really work if you needed to recover?

2. Have you tested using the most likely scenarios? Are these scenarios changed each test cycle, such as every year? Would it be prudent to adopt a different scenario for your next test?

3. Do you perform regular desktop exercises?

4. Do you document all issues, are they owned, and do they have a viable action plan? Do you track your actions to make sure that progress is being made? Do you have a process to escalate issues? If not, look at how you can embed appropriate action tracking into your processes.

5. Are your tests adequately resourced with suitably skilled people, and do you give everyone who could be involved the chance to gain experience?

6. Do you test frequently enough?

7. Are you identifying and managing the risks associated with testing?

8. Are test reports produced quickly and do they provide the stakeholders with the information they need?

9. Are your tests scripted so they cover the key operations that are required in recovery and the tests can be repeated?

10. Are users fully involved with the testing?

11. At the time you publish the final test report, do all the outstanding risks and issues have owners and action plans and are they set up so that they will be managed to completion after the test is closed?

Crisis Management Exercising

Things You Need to Know About Exercising

Crisis management exercises are all about giving the crisis management team a chance to experience in a safe environment the potential issues they could face so they can hone their skills, get used to their responsibilities, learn to work as a team, and test the details of their plans and any supporting facilities and tools. Typical exercises are conducted—with the whole team present—normally in the chosen crisis command room and in the form of a role play. Team members are informed of the background to the scenario being tested, then asked to operate as a team and respond in role as information is fed into the team by a facilitator

The scenarios generally relate to common impacts and so involve things such as the loss of a site, loss of IT, loss of staff, supplier failure, or something that threatens to damage the reputation of the organization. Exercises can range from very basic paper-based desktop exercises to very elaborate affairs with actors playing roles, mocked-up news reports, and physical relocation of the crisis team during the exercise to the recovery site or alternate crisis room.

Key Elements in Crisis Management Exercises

The key elements that contribute to a successful crisis management exercise are:

- Meaningful scenario
- Successful outcome for the people taking part
- Developing the crisis management team
- Improving the crisis management process
- Demonstrating the appropriateness of the materials
- Good input for the exercise
- Using timeouts
- Planning well
- Engaging management
- Conducting exercises frequently
- Reporting quickly and accurately
- Setting roles and responsibility

The majority of this chapter expands on these aspects of successful crisis management testing. The key purposes of the crisis exercise can be split between:

- Making sure that the crisis management process team and plan are effective
- Training the members of the crisis management team in their roles and the likely scenarios they could face

In general, crisis management exercises carry little risk, and as such they don't need the coordination of a variety of work streams or technical resources as you would see with disaster recovery (DR) and work area recovery (WAR) tests.

Most of the work involves preparing the scenario and organizing the actual exercise. Consequently, there's no need for the same focus on project management and planning that you have with IT DR and WAR tests.

Choose a Meaningful Crisis Scenario

The selection of the scenario has a direct effect on the extent and effectiveness of the crisis exercises, the development of the crisis team, and the improvement of the crisis management processes and plans.

The scenario should:

- Be consistent with the organization's most likely and highest-impact scenarios.

- Develop an enterprise-wide understanding of exposure to the key scenarios.

- Prepare the crisis leadership team to deal with a possible real-world crisis.

- Target any specific development needs that exist within the crisis team.

- Provide management with some insight into the key risks to which the organization is exposed.

- Help to justify the ongoing business continuity and DR program.

- Be progressive in that each subsequent exercise provides greater confidence in the effectiveness of crisis management and the viability of the recovery solution that underpins it.

If possible and sensible, I recommend that you align the exercises with the scenario being used for DR and WAR testing. If you haven't decided on a scenario for all DR and WAR tests, I'd recommend either:

- Selecting a realistic scenario that could lead to the greatest impact on your organization.

- Selecting a scenario that's topical within your organization, industry, or the world at large (e.g., a flu pandemic).

- Select a scenario that ensures the maximum number of participants are actively involved in the crisis response.

People Need a Successful Outcome

When selecting a scenario and preparing the exercise, it's critical that you pick something in which the crisis management team will ultimately be successful.

You can't plan how the team will respond to the scenario or the timing of all the inputs they will receive during the exercise. However, you should plan a viable outcome and, if the team starts to falter, you should redirect it toward this successful conclusion, making sure that the errors and deficiencies are captured.

Developing the Crisis Management Team

Managing a crisis successfully depends on having people with the right skills and the know how needed to respond to the types of events that an organization may face.

Modern organizations tend to be quite democratic, devolved, and distributed. They can operate with high degrees of autonomy and empowerment. But managing a crisis requires a simple command-and-control structure.

To successfully manage a crisis, you need someone who's in control and you need rapid communication of the salient information and the ability to quickly provide direction to those people who are required to act.

Because of these demands, it's important that the crisis management team is well rehearsed in their roles and responsibilities and all the lines of communication are fully tested.

Note   Command and control can be at odds with the normal way of operating your organization, so make sure you plan and train for it.

Improving the Crisis Management Process

One of your principal aims in conducting exercises is to improve the crisis management process. Your choice of scenarios and your choice of personnel influence the extent that the exercise will help you improve the overall process.

However, there will only be improvements if you take on board what you observe, fix the issues, and improve the processes after the exercise.

Don't be too hard on yourself; the process of improvement never really ends, although you should see the number of improvements steadily being reduced with each subsequent exercise.

Likewise, don't rest on your laurels, as a permanently stable environment is unknown in the real world. Things change, and hence you must keep looking for things you need to improve—in your plans, in your teams, in your relationships, in your communication, in your escalation, in your decision making, in your feedback loops, and in your solutions.

Make Sure Exercise Materials Are Appropriate

An easy mistake is to prepare the exercise for yourself, an exercise that you love but not one the customer of the exercise needs or can relate to. Make sure you engage with your stakeholders, especially the manager who is accountable for crisis management in your organization. Make sure that what you produce is aligned to your organization's expectations. Don't deliver an amazing multimedia exercise with a cast of thousands if what your organization believes is needed is a simple paper-based exercise with you providing the inputs from the front of the room.

Employ Quality Inputs to the Exercise

Inputs, or injects, as they are often called, are how you feed information into the exercise. Like materials, the inputs must be in keeping with expectations.

There are many choices when it comes to injects, which include:

- Phone inputs, where you get people to role play on incoming calls

- Handouts

- Visuals, where you put up the content of the input on a screen for everyone to read

- Role play, where people enter the room to deliver their input

- Business recovery teams, where the crisis management team consults the people responsible for doing the recovery actions and feeds back their responses to the crisis management team

- Directions, where you provide the input as an update to the exercise

- Media, where you provide inputs via simulated news flashes, radio broadcasts, Web pages, and so forth

The key thing is to keep in mind the scenario and overall goals of the exercise when you plan the inputs so you can identify inputs that will move the scenario forward or expose key risks and issues.

Don't be rigid once the exercise is under way. If an exercise inject is no longer valuable, don't just deliver it because you have prepared it. It can confuse the exercise and impair progress.

▧ **Tip** Be prepared to think on your feet. If things are stalling, improvise injects that will get them moving or take a time out to get the team refocused and back on schedule.

Use Timeouts

Timeouts—pauses in the middle of the crisis exercise—are invaluable as they provide an opportunity to:

- Reflect on progress

- Allow participants to step outside their roles and see events from different perspectives

- Reconsider the current approach and in particular assess if what they are doing is going to achieve a successful and expedient conclusion

- Reflect on key learnings from the exercise so far and record these learnings as actions to improve crisis management in the future

The format is simple. Just call the exercise to a temporary halt. Ideally everyone should be aware that you may call timeouts and what to expect.

Engage Management

Like any endeavor, your crisis management exercises will succeed or fail depending on the quality of your management engagement.

Unlike other projects, this has less to do with accountability and securing resources and everything to do with perception and input.

Make sure you have discussed at length the objectives of the exercise and that key management stakeholders agree with your approach and goals. Make sure you have dealt with all their concerns or objections and respectfully taken on board their input.

There should be no surprises, although the actual scenario may not be known if they have a role to perform. In other words, everyone should enter the session knowing what to expect, what they have to do, and how to do it, but unaware of the exact scenario or the inputs they will have to deal with.

Rotate Participants

Crisis management exercises are like WAR and DR tests in that you may want to include the alternates and not just the principal players. Basically, for each role on the crisis management team you should have a primary person and some named backups who can cover if the primary is unavailable. Using these alternates during the exercise helps to test whether the plan is fit for a specific purpose. Having different people involved can also provide a fresh perspective on the process and how it could be improved.

When you use inexperienced people, you should make sure they have support. You don't want them to fail. What you do want is to flush out any issues with the plan or with the recovery strategy and, wherever possible, fix these things as you go along.

Ideally, each time you test you want to have a mix of primary and backup people in play, much as you'd see on any real working day.

One of the keys is to track who has been involved in exercises and make sure that over time everyone gets an opportunity to take part and perform their allocated role. You might want to allow backup resources to observe. This is up to you, but if you do, there needs to be some basic ground rules in place. For example, they can stay in the room but they may not engage with anyone.

Conduct Crisis Exercises Frequently

For testing to be effective, it must be conducted regularly. The frequency is a balance between benefits and costs.

In practice, it's hard to persuade managers to schedule exercises more than once a year. However, if you leave it go for much more than a year, the chances of problems emerging increase significantly, as do the gaps in the knowledge of your crisis management team.

Like DR and WAR, I recommend making regular crisis management exercises a key element of your policy supported by written standards.

I include some high-level policy statement, such as "Crisis management exercises must be carried out at least annually," in the policy. Then, in the standards, set out exactly what constitutes an exercise, what reports should be produced, and so on. Add guidelines such as "All primary role holders must have been involved in an exercise in the past 2 years" and "All role holders must be briefed on their roles and responsibilities."

Of course, you need to do what is normal for your organization, unless doing nothing is normal, in which case do break with tradition and do something! However, if there are no standards as such in your organization, then put it all in the policy.

Report Frequently and Accurately

There's little point exercising if you don't capture the key lessons, create a set of actions, and share it with the key stakeholders.

As with the other tests, there are three audiences for testing reports:

- Management, who wants assurances that everything is okay and that you can or have fixed issues that came up.

- Technical staff, who wants to know exactly what the issues are, what's agreed upon, and who is responsible for fixing the issues.

- Auditors and control functions, which indicate whether appropriate controls are in place and that you are identifying and managing breaches. They will also want to see that the tests are being conducted in keeping with your internal controls (i.e., your policy).

I find it good practice to have a single report issued within a month of the test. Unlike DR and WAR, I don't advocate a flash report for crisis exercises, but this is a personal preference.

The single report is dependent on a postexercise meeting, where all the issues should be discussed and actions and owners agreed upon. The report sets out all the issues, actions, timescales, and recommendations. Plan to take up to 2 weeks to pull together the report for a large exercise.

Exercise Roles and Responsibilities

Roles and responsibilities can be split among:

- Preparation
- Exercise management
- Exercise participation
- Observation
- Issue fix

Preparatory Roles and Responsibilities

Unlike DR and WAR, the majority of the preparation for an exercise is not about risk avoidance and clearing old issues. However, like WAR and DR, about 80% of the work that makes up a test involves the preparation, mainly focused on designing the exercise and preparing the materials. Key activities include:

- Selecting the scenario, including goals and learning outcomes.

- Writing out the scenario.

- Preparing materials and inputs.

- Briefing all the people who will assist with the exercise, like those creating exercise inputs, etc.

- Conducting walkthroughs to iron out issues with the flow, timing, etc.

- Fixing issues that may be lingering from earlier exercises.

- Training and briefing new crisis management team members on their roles and responsibilities.

The majority of this work is undertaken by the business continuity manager, unless you are lucky enough to have some dedicated crisis management people.

Exercise Management

After all the hard work preparing the exercise, it would be tragic to leave the day to chance, so good leadership and control of the exercise are essential.

This depends on:

- The preparation you have done

- The details of the scenario

- How familiar you are with the scenario details and the context within the organization

It's also linked to your willingness to follow what you have prepared. Avoid winging it at all costs, but always be on the lookout for the unexpected or slippages and be prepared to adapt your plans as you go.

Tip Doing dry runs is an excellent way of preparing. Do it first on your own, then get some other people in. It's amazing how quickly you can come to realize how your excellent written word comes out sounding affected or wooden, or how the scenario just doesn't flow or has too many injects for the time allowed.

Trust me, no matter how good you are at preparing scenarios, there will be plenty of areas that can be improved and probably some that are just plain awful. Better to find this out doing a dry run than in front of the board of your company!

The quality of materials is also a key factor, so the advice again is to try them out first. Don't just trust your judgment; run them past as many people as possible early on. Don't be shy, and remember nobody is perfect, but the best people iron out the creases in their work at their leisure.

Exercise Participation

We've touched on rotation of personnel and ensuring that the backup people get a chance to sit in the hot seat.

The other thing to ensure is that you have all roles filled. The exercise will falter if, say, your IT crisis team member doesn't show up.

When planning an exercise, be both empathetic to the fact that people are busy but also unequivocal about the need for people to attend. If they can't commit the time, then drop them as a team member; they are of no benefit to you.

Something else you have to weigh as you look at participants is whether they really are the right people to undertake their responsibilities. Just because your chief operating officer is accountable for crisis management doesn't mean he's the best person to take on the role of crisis leader. This is a tough call, but, not having the right people in place if a disaster strikes will be far tougher.

Observation Roles and Responsibilities

As part of the exercise, you need to establish:

- That people actually do what the plan says. If not, then either their behavior needs to change or the plan needs to change.

- That the crisis team has the talent, skills, and knowledge to discharge their responsibilities.

- Whether there are any issues with the current plan, people, processes, controls, resources, or tools.

- Whether there are any ways that the crisis management process or materials can be improved.

In my experience, just as with DR and WAR technicians, members of the crisis management team rarely follow the plans. That's because they get their adrenaline up and leap into action.

This is a key thing to observe, and it's a key thing to focus on when you call your timeouts. Redirecting people back to their plans, like any directions offered in the timeout, is best done in a coaching style. Ask questions and get people to identify the issue and reiterate to you what they should be doing.

Again, like technicians, members of the crisis management team are often quite bad at ensuring that the steps they actually perform are included in the plans. One of the planning assumptions should always be that the key people are unavailable, so plans must be written so that any competent business manager could perform the crisis management responsibilities.

Keeping records of what people do, what doesn't work, or how long things take is important, but it shouldn't be as much of an issue as it is for IT DR or WAR exercises. In general, much of the detail is captured in any case. It should be someone on the crisis management team's responsibility to scribe for the team, and issues, actions, and timings are among the key things that should be recorded by the scribe. But you need to observe how effective the scribe is and how well the information is used by the crisis leader and the rest of the crisis management team.

Keep your eyes open for improvements, note them, and either feed them back during timeout or include them in the posttest review or final reporting.

Just like with DR and WAR, you must select the people for observation with care. They need to have an eye for detail, great people skills, and thick skin. They also need to be confident working with the senior people who make up your crisis management team.

With regard to observation, you should also bear in mind it's very hard to be an objective or comprehensive observer if you have a significant role in the actual exercise, such as being a member of the crisis team responding to the scenario or as the facilitator who is delivering the exercise.

Issue Fix Roles and Responsibilities

There's little point in testing if you're not going to address any issues that emerge.

Have patience when it comes to discovering new and unknown issues that undermine the viability of your crisis management team, their plans, or materials. Don't be tolerant when it comes to discovering an issue that still exists from an earlier exercise.

Consequently, I recommend that for any issue:

- You identify the person or group that can fix it.

- Senior managers who control these resources are made accountable for the issue's timely resolution.

- Resources are allocated, work planned, and realistic timescales are agreed upon to fix the issue.

- You review general progress and progress against the timescales regularly.

- You escalate any failure to progress immediately.

In terms of roles and responsibilities, I'd recommend that:

- The continuity manager tracks all issues centrally and regularly reviews progress.

- Those performing the fix are made aware of the timelines and visibility of the issue.

- The accountable managers are held accountable for reasonable progress.

Closing a Crisis Exercise

The production of the final report does not signify the end of the exercise. But you do need to make a formal distinction between the exercise as a project and ongoing business-as-usual activities.

There's a danger that your tests can lack a clear endpoint, with issues being managed for months or years after the actual tests.

It's thus important to draw an end to the project and transition any lingering issues into business-as-usual issue management so that nothing gets lost but you can move on.

The key thing is to ensure that all actions are owned and they continue to be tracked but not as part of the project. In addition to outstanding issues, you need to ensure that everything the organization learned as part of the test is being used to its fullest.

Finally, you have to move the people who have been working on the crisis exercise project back to their normal roles or other projects, and in doing this, it's very important that you provide them and their managers with feedback on their performance, contribution, and behaviors. This final people point is often overlooked and people fail to capitalize on the development opportunity or recognition for their efforts.

Action Plan

Review the following questions and consider if you need to follow the recommendations:

1. If you tested services and solutions, how confident are you that these would really work if you needed to recover?

2. Have you tested using the most likely scenarios? Are these scenarios changed every year? Would it be prudent to adopt a different scenario for your next exercise?

3. Do you perform regular desktop exercises?

4. Are all the issues documented, owned, and lead to a viable action plan? Do you track your actions to make sure that progress is being made? Do you have a process to escalate issues? If not, then look at how you can embed appropriate action tracking into your processes.

5. Are your tests adequately resourced with suitably skilled people? Do you give everyone who could be involved the chance to gain experience?

6. Do you test frequently enough?

7. Are you identifying and managing the risks associated with the exercises?

8. Are exercise reports produced quickly and do they provide the stakeholders with the information they need?

9. Are your exercises scripted so they cover the key operations that are required in recovery and the exercises can be repeated?

10. Are users fully involved with the exercises?

11. At the time you publish the final exercise report, do all the outstanding risks and issues have owners and action plans and are they set up so they will be managed to completion after the exercise is formally closed?

Maintenance

Maintaining Your Plans, Solutions, and Skills

Maintaining your plans and solutions is essential if your recovery plan is going to work on the day you need it to. This chapter sets out what you'll need to do to maintain a plan and the best way to go about it.

Never Forget: Disaster Recovery Is an Essential Function

The most important principle to grasp—and to promote in your organization—is that disaster recovery (DR) is a part of any production capability. When I say DR, I really mean all recovery solutions, so this applies to business recovery as well as IT.

There's a tendency for organizations to treat DR in the same way they treat their IT development and IT testing. In other words, it's treated as noncritical. And like many noncritical activities, DR is often outside any formal change controls. In other words, if a significant change is planned or occurs, DR plans aren't automatically updated to reflect the change.

A multitude of issues arise whenever changes to the production environment are dealt with separately from DR or WAR (work area recovery). Inevitably, when there are poor controls, production and your recovery solutions get out of step, and, once out of step, they can't be relied on.

If you find that every time you prepare a test you are sweeping up changes from the production environment and updating your recovery solutions, then clearly you have a major problem. Obviously, this is unacceptable because of the risk it entails. However, from an operating perspective, it highlights a major inefficiency as the cost of applying all of these changes twice is considerably more than doing it once.

> ▦ **Tip** Work to make sure any changes in the production environment are reflected, in close to real time, in your DR plan.

Review Change Management Processes and Controls

It's essential that business and IT recovery is covered by your organization's change process and controls. Don't go reinventing the wheel! The basics that you need to have in place are:

- Employ gateway controls. At each stage of your change process, you should have a check to make sure business continuity and DR have been included in any changes.

- Avoid the "Is business continuity impacted by this change, yes or no?" type of questions. It's too easy for people who don't appreciate the impact or who just want to bypass it to answer "No."

- Make it harder to get changes through that don't impact business continuity by requiring any exceptions (i.e., things that don't impact WAR or DR) to be approved by the product or service owner.

- Make gateways formal. It's not good enough to just include business continuity in a checklist. Any changes need to be formally signed off.

- Never lose sight of accountability. Whoever is accountable for production should also be accountable for DR in that area and also held accountable when and where gaps become apparent.

- Those responsible for making changes need to be made aware that business continuity and DR are part of their responsibilities.

Identify Events that Trigger Business Continuity Management Reviews

Many changes become apparent when you prepare for the annual test. This, again, highlights the risk that when you need to invoke DR plans, they won't work. In addition to changes in management, it's worth identifying trigger events that require a review of business continuity. Good examples that might constitute a trigger event include:

- When production volumes change by more than 40%
- When staff increases by more than 30%
- When revenue increases by 50%
- When the main processing is moved offshore

These are common examples, but the exact trigger events must be relevant to your business.

Use the trigger event to review the business continuity provisions. For example, if staff increases, do you still have enough seats in an alternate worksite? Will they be available soon enough? Or if sales increase, will the existing IT infrastructure or telephony still support the required volumes? As you'll discover, trigger events are an excellent way of integrating business changes into your continuity plans as they happen.

Make sure trigger events are included in the business continuity policy. The responsibility for acting on trigger events should also be specifically stated in the job description or objectives for business continuity coordinators and the accountable managers. And it's not for business continuity to identify the changes that trigger plan reviews; the department or division must identify them.

Tip Set a time limit on trigger events. For example, policy should state that a review must be initiated within 30 days of the business change.

When a planned activity leads to change, it's easy to keep in mind your responsibilities to revisit continuity plans. But often you'll experience the creeping change that comes about through organic or compound growth. If volumes grow 10% a year, it won't take long before the business outgrows its business continuity provisions. This sort of creeping change is less a matter for a trigger event and more a matter of something that needs to be reviewed at least annually as part of the normal business reviews.

Maintain Your Business Continuity Plan

In addition to any reviews that are initiated as a consequence of a trigger event, schedule regular reviews of all the business continuity plans.

I'd recommend that these reviews be planned to follow from the business impact analysis, as the business impact analysis (BIA) will almost certainly identify changes that need to be incorporated into your plans. So, by doing them together, you can kill two birds with one stone.

I'd also recommend that the best timing for reviews is agreed upon through consultation with the business areas in question. I find it easiest to walk through the latest BIA and then discuss whether the business continuity plan is still appropriate based on how the BIA has changed from the previous year.

I also walk through the plan with the business continuity coordinator and ideally with the accountable manager to see if it's still accurate, practical, and easily understood. I strongly advise that you don't simply delegate this important meeting to the business coordinator, as that person can often be blind to what's actually in the plan and won't always see gaps or weaknesses that will come out through a facilitated desk review.

Business Recovery Solution Maintenance

Through tests and regular business continuity plan reviews, you should be able to identify changes you need to make to keep the work area recovery solution current.

In addition, I'd recommend doing an annual review of the WAR arrangements. Look at the site, facilities, server rooms, telephony, and network connections and think about what change is likely over the next 3 years. Start to plan or at least debate the necessary upgrades.

With third-party arrangements, you always need to be mindful of the duration of the contract and any contractual break points, because if you need to change locations or have some other major change, you'll want to align this with the break points in your contracts.

Maintain Your Information Technology Disaster Recovery Solution

As with WAR, DR should be change controlled, and anything that slips through the net should get swept up when you test.

Again like WAR, if you use a third party, think about how your business is changing and how you can manage this change most effectively within the constraints of the contract.

Maintain Your Crisis Management Plan

Your crisis management plans should be reviewed at least every quarter and new copies of the changed sections circulated. If you work in a larger organization, you'll probably find that your crisis management team and key contacts will come and go, and if you wait much more than a few months to update this, the plan will look out of date and leave you exposed.

As a general rule, I'd walk through all the documents that make up the crisis management plan, paying special attention to the contacts, at least once a quarter.

Maintain Your Policies

You will probably have some rules in your organization about reviewing your policies. As guidance, I'd recommend reviewing the policy once every 2 years. As a rule, the policy should be quite static, although you may find that in the first few years it evolves quite quickly as you extend and refine it.

Tip   Review your work area recovery plan at least annually, your crisis management plan at least quarterly, and your business continuity polices at least every 2 years.

Action Plan

Review the following questions before progressing and consider the recommendations:

- Is DR included as part of the change management process? If not, then review your change process and make sure you have the basics in place.

- Have you identified trigger events that, if they occur, indicate that it's time for some relevant maintenance activity?

- Have you embedded the maintenance of all your business continuity documents, policies, reports, tools, and solutions into your business-as-usual processes?

Execute the Plan

Manage a Disaster

How to Respond When a Disaster Strikes

There are three decisive things about business survival: how you manage the events you face, how you make decisions, and how you monitor your responses.

This chapter explains command and control in a disaster and helps you to set up a crisis management team that will get you out of the tightest squeeze.

Identification and Notification

There's no point in having a plan or a solution if you fail to notice that you have had an incident!

Nearly as bad as total ignorance is not picking up on an incident until it has become a full-scale disaster. With timely action, most incidents can be managed without leading to a full-blown disaster. However, many seemingly minor incidents can develop into major problems that can ultimately destroy organizations if people are not paying attention.

So, clearly you need to monitor minor incidents and make sure they don't escalate into major incidents.

Identifying Incidents

Incidents come in all shapes and sizes, and you can't predict them all. Chances are that for every possible incident, there will be someone in your organization who was aware of the underlying activity. For example, someone notices a leak in the water main in the basement on Monday, then forgets about it until Thursday, when the trickle becomes a torrent.

What we have to do is join up the eyes and ears of your organization and train people to look for the relevant signs.

Some areas, like IT and facilities, will probably be quite mature, with established protocols, procedures, and so forth. This is good news because these are the two areas most likely to have major incidents that can lead you to invoke your recovery plans. However, other areas are often not as mature, such as in the production areas where business process failures are probably managed locally and in isolation.

In that case, I'd recommend the following steps:

1. Identify what incident processes already exist.

2. Establish a consistent way of assessing the impact and rating it. For example, the loss of a data center, building, or critical supplier would be category 1, loss of a major system would be category 2, loss of minor system would be category 3, etc.

3. Set some trigger points for the areas that are managing localized events. The trigger points indicate when you must notify the business continuity manager or incident manager that an event has occurred. For example, you might decide that the designated person should be notified immediately in person if a category 1 incident occurs. If a category 2 incident occurs, you notify by e-mail, and so forth.

If you identify an incident that is critical enough to require recovery, then initiate the recovery steps. Don't wait for approval or second opinions. Of course, you must make this a matter of policy or have preagreement that you have authority to respond in this fashion.

You also need to empower those people who will be in a position of response so they too can act as required.

Having put in place processes, triggers, policies, and associated authority, all that remains is to train the people. Hence my suggestion is that you exercise, exercise, exercise—and make sure you involve management so there are no surprises, there's no lost time, and there are no repercussions afterward.

Most invocation decisions don't have an immediate effect and are quickly reversible. However, it's worth understanding the impact of each step so you can include some checkpoints or gateways if you feel the need.

Tip   If an incident is critical enough to require recovery, initiate the recovery steps immediately. Don't wait for approval or ask for the opinion of others. Move. Now. Of course, your policy should have permitted you to act when necessary without oversight.

Monitoring Incidents

Now, assuming that you have the basic notification process in place, the next step is to monitor progress and assess whether the incident is being managed effectively or requires escalation.

If it becomes clear that the incident is not being managed effectively or plans are not having the desired impact, escalate the incident to higher authorities to ensure action is taken. Don't delay; escalate as soon as you see a lack of control or a lack of progress.

I can't emphasize this enough. Time is like sand: once it slips through your fingers it's gone forever. When it comes to recovery, you have a fixed time that it takes to recover, and there's probably very little time for delay, so don't!

Triage

Just as in a hospital's accident and emergency department, you have to sort out the life-threatening incidents from the minor irritations. Just as in an emergency room, you have to do it quickly. Then focus on the life-and-death situations first before attending to the walking wounded.

From a business incident point of view, rather than waiting for someone like you to assess the incident, you want the business to self-assess the incident as it occurs. It's a bit like patients assessing whether they need to go to the emergency room or stay at home and take an aspirin.

This should be an area of focus for your education and awareness program. It should be a key focus for all people who are in a position of being first responders, including those likely to spot emerging issues or who are the first to deal with them.

The first thing you need to do is identify the "no-brainers." Security should never phone you up to say, "A helicopter just hit the roof. What should we do?" They should start the plan rolling first and make people aware as the plan or crisis management process dictates.

A little frivolous perhaps, but you get the point. You should have identified the no-brainers like this as defined by the few possible outcomes and have clear instructions for all responders.

Just as with risk analysis, focus on outcomes and not possible causes. So, your security guard is responding to the outcome that the office block is not available, thus, he has invoked the building recovery plan.

Focusing on outcomes makes it much simpler as you reduce these down to between five and seven possible outcomes, and as students of psychology will tell you, seven is a good number of things as it corresponds to the amount of items an average person can remember. Note: Don't rely on people's memory; make sure it's all documented.

Tip When a disaster strikes, don't give any thought to causes. There will be plenty of time later to do that. Instead, focus on managing the outcomes of the disaster. "The building is on fire? We must get people out immediately, and then invoke WAR."

Command and Control

Once the crisis response is in action, you should quickly establish a command-and-control structure.

Generally, this is the domain of the crisis management team and its process.

Unlike normal business operations, when in crisis mode, there should be a more rigid command-and-control structure, with short lines of communication, near real-time flow of information, and rapid decision making.

However, you should make sure all the individuals with recovery roles are empowered to act within their responsibilities. There should be some boundaries around their autonomy in that:

- They shouldn't start until given clear instruction or they can clearly establish that it's okay to begin.

- They should report progress and issues and seek direction when issues arise if they are material and when questions are delaying their progress or risk the quality of the outcome.

To maximize command-and-control efficiency, meetings should be brief. They should be managed by the leader at that level in the command hierarchy. Crisis meetings should follow a preagreed-upon agenda along the lines of:

- New developments or changes in context

- Issues

- Progress against an agreed-upon action plan
- Next steps
- Time of next meeting or any other business

The leader should hold court and may want to go around the room (or call if it's a virtual meeting) and get each member to provide an update on each topic. I find focusing on one area at a time works best when each member of the team runs through the agenda as it applies to their area. Keep them to a couple of minutes each.

You need to be disciplined and limit people's time and keep them focused on things that are salient to the group as a whole. Some people forget this and start recounting trivia.

If people can't communicate salient information quickly, then they lack one of the most important skills for members of a crisis management team: brevity!

You should have scribes and keep the salient information visible at all times. I like to use whiteboards arranged so that everyone in the room can see them. I'd recommend keeping up-to-date event, issues, actions, and risk logs in electronic form so they can be reviewed by anyone not in the room.

Then, as soon as you've gone around the room with all the members, established the facts, and decided on the next steps, you should immediately conclude the meeting to let people get on with their tasks and meet again as agreed.

This meeting will be repeated at the next lower level of the hierarchy, where each crisis team member convenes his or her respective teams and briefs them on what was decided and initiates the next steps in the recovery for their area. Again, this should be brief with a focus on cascading the salient information to the team, capturing feedback, and getting everyone focused on the immediate priorities.

The Leader's Job

When running the crisis meetings, the leader should direct things. It's important to maintain momentum, focusing on the agenda while making sure balance is maintained. The leader will find it useful to work through the whiteboards or whatever was used to record events, issues, and actions. The leader should ask for specific updates if he or she hasn't heard enough about a particular topic, and, if necessary, detail someone to investigate it further.

The crisis leader needs to be constantly assessing whether the plan is progressing, whether prescribed actions are working, and, if not, what should be done to bring the recovery back on plan. The leader also needs to review what people are actually doing and weigh reality against what they should be doing. In other words, evaluating "what the plan says they should be doing" vs. "what they are doing." Where there are gaps between plans and reality, the leader needs to understand why and be assured that it's justified and appropriate.

Leaders need to look at the team and make sure they are giving people the right direction and support. It is of no value to just shout at people—leaders have to be sure people understand and are in a good frame of mind to get the job done.

In a crisis situation, it's essential that the crisis leader demonstrates calmness and a positive focus. The leader needs to redirect people away from the issues (past) and channel them toward positive action (present). Everyone needs to be clear about who's in charge and remain confident that things will work out.

■ **Tip** In a midst of a crisis, help people focus on taking positive action in the present, rather than rehashing issues related to the past.

Records

You should provide all your recovery teams, including the crisis management team, with templates for event, issues, actions, and risk logs. However, in a crisis it's not just about having a record of these things; the critical thing is that everyone can see them.

I've been in too many exercises where the scribe simply keys everything into a computer. They have a perfect and instant record, but it's quite useless because nobody else can see it.

It is far better to record all the salient facts on whiteboards that everyone in the room can see.

The scribe can easily type these notes up as soon as the meeting concludes or even after the incident.

Postmortem

Once the incident is resolved, it's important that the key people review:

- The identification of the incident
- Incident escalation
- Invocation of the plans
- Effectiveness of the plans

- Adherence to the plans, processes, and controls
- Quality of the meetings
- Communication
- Performance of key areas and personnel
- Records, scribing, and administrative support
- Issues and risks
- Return to normal operations
- Closure of the incident

The postmortem meeting should be formal and result in an agreed-upon action plan with clear ownership and target dates.

Last but not least, the action plan as a whole must be owned; someone must make sure that it has been completed.

It's normally the business continuity manager who will track progress against the actions and monitor risks. However, it should be a far more senior manager who owns the overall plan and is ultimately responsible for its completion.

Responding to Different Scenarios

We have covered the generic elements of managing an event, and in your preparation you should have considered a range of scenarios and ideally practiced your responses with these in mind.

Now it's time to dive a little deeper into some of the most likely scenarios you might face.

Responding to Loss of Technology

Technology failure—and the loss of IT systems in particular—is one of the most likely events that can lead to disaster.

With luck, before disaster strikes you will have had time to identify your most critical services, prepare recovery strategies, and worked out the correct order to recover them. Having done all that, you should have the documentation ready and trained all the staff who need to be involved in a recovery (see Chapter 5 for a full explanation from a systems perspective).

With technology, time is often critical. In many cases, the difference between the maximum tolerable period of disruption (MTPD) and how long it will actually take to recover the system is quite small. This means that, in practice, there's little time for delays when making the decision to invoke, getting staff in a position to undertake the recovery, addressing issues and problems that may emerge, among others.

So act quickly. If you're unsure, initiate the recovery. You can always stand down later.

A particular mistake you must avoid is waiting until all available options have been exhausted. By this I mean trying to fix it. It's easy to keep trying one more thing or to wait a few more minutes.

Instead, think about DR and fixing the problem as parallel activities. Initiate your DR while you're still trying to fix the problems. That way you won't lose time, and then if you do exhaust all the possibilities for recovery, your DR will be well under way. Also, you may find that DR gets to a point where it's ready while you're still working on the fix, which will give you another option to consider.

You also need to think slightly differently if your DR solution is delivered via a third party. If it is, you want to avoid being beaten to any shared resources by another business that needs to invoke.

Bear in mind that most third-party suppliers allow you to put them on standby for securing your systems. They start clearing the site down to make it ready for you, which normally takes up to 4 hours and involves freeing up any resources that are currently being used for testing by other DR customers.

There's normally a cost associated with this, and the cost will be incurred regardless of whether you finally decide to invoke. There will also probably be a daily usage charge. Hence, to be sure you can act quickly, you need to have already secured the authority. You really don't want to be wasting time trying to find someone who can approve the expenditure at three in the morning—or indeed at any time—because time is slipping through your fingers and you will not be able to recover it.

When recovering your systems, you have to allow some time to test them before unleashing them on the users. The last thing you want to do is bring up the wrong system, or wrong data, or corrupt the live data.

Testing shouldn't take long and should have been a consideration when preparing your recovery plan. It should be documented in the plan, and you should make sure you get suitable approval before letting users on. This is good practice and also protects your critical systems.

If you don't have a recovery strategy, you will need to start from scratch, procure some hardware, find somewhere to put it that has appropriate environmental support, build the operating systems, build the applications, and restore the data.

The odds are against recovering if you're not prepared. Trying to recover your IT without DR is like planning your retirement by buying lottery tickets each week.

Even if you could get something up and running, how much data will you have lost? If you don't have a decent backup strategy, at best it could be days or weeks of data lost and at worst it could be all your data and proprietary software too!

I'd suggest that if you fail to recover your major systems, then in a matter of weeks, rather than months, your business will fail.

Tip   No matter what it takes, have an IT disaster recovery plan in place. If you fail to recover your major systems because you did not plan, the penalty could be the worst imaginable—failure of the business itself.

Responding to a Loss of a Building

Assuming you have some strategy for dealing with the loss of a critical building and you have prepared and rehearsed the plans, it should be a relatively smooth process to maintain operations without the building in question.

Just as for IT DR, invoking your building recovery is time critical for exactly the same reasons. You have a limited amount of spare time between how long it actually takes and how long before it's needed.

Just as for DR, you also need to think slightly differently where your recovery solution is delivered via a third-party provider. If it is, you want to avoid the possibility of being beaten to it by another business that also needs to invoke.

Again, most WAR suppliers allow you to put them on standby, allowing you to secure your positions. They start getting the site ready for you in case you need it.

Like for DR, there's normally a cost associated with placing the supplier on standby, and this cost will be incurred regardless of whether you finally decide to invoke. There will also be a daily usage charge that is levied for every single day you make use of the facility.

To ensure that you can act quickly, make sure that you secure the authority to invoke in advance.

If you don't have a recovery solution in place, you will need to act quickly, secure what facilities you can, mobilize your IT staff, and work like dogs. Not wanting to be the voice of doom, but if you're not prepared, the odds are not good. Basically, the majority of organizations that fail to recover following a major incident tend to go out of business in a relatively short time!

The good news is that if you manage an effective recovery, then the statistics demonstrate that you will most likely see an increase in shareholder value.

Even for less critical activities, you will sooner or later need to find somewhere or some way to get them done.

I deal with WAR and other strategies fully in Chapter 6.

Responding to a Denial of Access to a Building

More likely than the scenario in which you lose your building is the one where you find that your staff is not allowed into their place of work. This is most often the result of either a false alarm, like a defective fire alarm, or because of a localized event like a power failure.

In the majority of cases, these events are resolved quickly. So, it's important you don't let your staff stray off too far, as you'll want to be able to bring them back to work as quickly as possible.

To do this you need to have:

- Marshaling points
- Evacuation plans
- Trained marshals
- Simple lines of communication
- Staff that knows what to do and where to go

Marshaling Points

Marshaling points are prearranged places where staff are directed to meet if the building is evacuated. Ideally, they should be near to your building, but far enough away if the situation was dangerous and an exclusion zone was imposed. Example: you have a bomb threat.

You may approach this in one of two ways:

- Have a primary marshaling point and a secondary one that you can fall back on if there's an exclusion zone. For example, the square opposite your building might be a primary marshaling point, and a park 800 yards away could be your secondary marshaling point.

- Select a single marshaling point that would be outside the likely exclusion zone for your building. Check with your emergency services for advice on this as it varies from place to place, but 250 yards is normally recommended.

A word of warning: you need to coordinate your plans with the surrounding offices. If the square opposite has room for 500 people, but there are ten buildings that all assume they will assemble their combined 5,000 staff there, you will have a major problem.

In general it's a good idea to work closely with your peers in other companies and locations. Share ideas, share information, and build relationships so you can offer one another support in a crisis. Plus, you can learn a lot from how others manage DR.

Evacuation Plan

Just like your broader business continuity planning, you need to consider the likely outcomes of having to evacuate. Then you should prepare a plan that can cater to what is likely to happen.

The plan must be simple, clear, and intuitive, so that everyone can understand it, remember it, and use it when required.

The plan should set out:

- Where staff will assemble
- How to evacuate the building
- How to account for staff
- How to establish if it's safe to return into the building
- How to communicate to staff

Trained Marshals

To make the evacuation safe and effective, you need trained marshals who will guide people from the building, make sure everyone gets out, perform a roll call, provide information to those coordinating the event, and cascade information back to the staff.

Marshals need basic training on the drill and likely scenarios. This should be supported by simple instructions and copies of the relevant plans.

You can do this by having them participate in actual drills. Ideally, they should observe another marshal the first time, then take on the role in subsequent drills. I'd also recommend having one-off training as part of the induction of new marshals, as well as periodic refresher courses.

It doesn't really matter how you do it. What matters is that these staff know what they have to do and will perform well if a situation arises.

Simple Lines of Communication

If you are to keep control of the situation, you will need to keep control of your staff. This is aided by having some basics rules, such as "Staff are to report to the muster points and await further instructions." Once you get staff at the muster point, it's a good idea to keep them apprised of what has happened. For example, "This is just a drill and we will be going back in soon."

You should think in advance of the best way to repopulate the building after an evacuation. It's a good idea to call people back in phases rather than just having everyone swamp the building in one instant.

To do this, you need to be able to get the message out to each muster point and get people to come back in the order you want. Maybe focus on getting critical staff back in first, like your call center operators and computer operators. Or maybe you bring the people back in an order that maximizes the smooth flow of people coming in, such as top floors first.

To do this, you'll need good lines of communication and good plans that cover who is where and who you should prioritize for a return to work.

You might find that it helps to arrange the muster points so that those most critical are nearest to the entrance.

Clearly, it's a good idea to provide the marshals who are at the muster points with walkie-talkies or runners so they can communicate with whomever is controlling the incident.

If the event is not a false alarm, and people have been stood down to wait for directions or sent home for the day, you will still need to contact people quickly. You will therefore have to invoke your call cascade plans and provide news to staff information lines.

The information lines can be used to post generic information about the incident and should not contain anything that is commercially sensitive as you have limited control about who can access this type of information.

Ideally, you might have the benefit of an automated call notification system, which will send any message you like to select groups of employees using many different means. It will try the home phone number, work mobile number, personal mobile, Blackberry, spouse's number, among others.

Staff Awareness

It's not just about training your crisis management team and the marshals. It's almost as important that every staff member knows where to go, what to do when they get there, what to expect, how to find out information, and what not to do.

Ideally, this should be covered in everyone's company induction. Every member of staff should have basic instructions sent to them that cover the evacuation drill, muster points, the basics of the crisis management plan, and key contacts.

Responding to the Loss of Key Staff

Loss of key staff covers all the things that can lead to a situation where key staff are unable to attend the place of work.

Increasingly, the focus of business continuity plans is the pandemic-type scenario where your staff stay away from your office in large numbers.

This is not unique to a pandemic; it could be due to more mundane things like bad weather, strikes, or school closures. In fact, these scenarios are more likely than a pandemic, which happens about once every 30 or 40 years. The difference with a pandemic is the duration and moral aspects of the scenario.

Think Skills and Tasks, *Not* Functions

Loss of key staff is a subtle and difficult scenario to deal with, and it can require considerable extra work to model the impact. Unlike most other scenarios, where you are thinking and acting at a function level—for example, "Facilities"—with this scenario, you need to consider individual tasks and the skills needed to complete them (e.g., "Maintaining the power supply.").

The first step is to identify key activities and the skills needed to do them. Then you need to look at where the biggest exposures are.

In this context, the biggest exposures are those things that depend on a single person, and then there are those that only a few people can do.

A big problem with this, and something you need to avoid, is being lulled by statistics. You might assume that 50% of your staff will be unavailable for the peak period of disruption, but this 50% will rarely be distributed evenly. So, you might have everyone in from the canteen but none of them can undertake the mandatory obligations of your company.

┌───┐
│   **HEARTS AND MINDS**   │
└───┘

I used to work with a DR manager who was always keen to point out that if something happened that put his family at risk, he'd put them first. His frankness kept me real, as it's all too easy to get caught up in the abstractness of plans. At the end of the day, it all comes down to people and in particular what people are thinking.

So, there's a school of thought that says you need to change what people think about coming to work. You need to give them assurances that work is actually not a dangerous place to go. Implementing a rigorous hygiene cleaning routine can be very effective and can provide other tangible benefits.

During the SARS outbreak, Barclays Capital introduced new cleaning procedures for their offices in Southeast Asia that included regular wiping down of all common surfaces. As a result, they saw a significant reduction in days lost from sickness that more than compensated for the additional cleaning costs.

You need to consider giving your staff access to better care as well. Many organizations offer their staff access to antiviral medicines, health screening, counseling, and support. You also need to make sure that staff get accurate information and not just the sensational scare stories from the media.

You need to consider the types of concerns your staff will have that will stop them from coming to work. Could it be public transport? You could put critical staff up in hotels, arrange taxis, or staff buses.

Split-Site Strategy

Some businesses advocate adopting a split-site strategy in certain situations. Take, for example, a pandemic. The idea is that you run your production and recovery site in parallel and split your people between the two sites in the hope of isolating them and offering staff a choice of locations.

In practice, I wouldn't recommend split site for such scenarios, because it adds complexity, and I don't believe it mitigates the risk of infection. Your staff will probably pick up the infection from their children or friends and the distribution of infection will be consistent regardless of location.

However, what split-site working will do is stretch your already stretched resources because you'll need to support two locations rather than just one!

Responding to the Loss of a Supplier

This covers all situations where a supplier is unable to provide critical services, products, or resources.

In recent years there has been a massive shift, especially among large corporations, where many of the traditional business functions have been outsourced. In many organizations, it is only those core activities that make that organization unique that are still done in house by their own staff.

Now the upside of outsourcing is that it brings greater focus to an organization and also brings better processes, know how, and economies of scale to areas like personnel, finance, catering, and facilities—things that an organization may not currently be all that good at.

However, it also brings a risk! So keep in mind that, although outsourced processes might not be core to your business, if these functions fail, then in some cases the whole organization can fail.

In short you need to understand your dependencies on suppliers. Where there's a need to recover or protect a function, you need to make that clear in your negotiations. It needs to be documented in the contract and you need to test it or see solid evidence that the supplier can meet its obligations to you.

You also need to keep a close eye on your suppliers. If they fail, you must act to secure an alternative supplier or, if at all possible, insource it.

Action Plan

Before moving on, reflect on the following questions and recommendations:

1. Are incidents in your organization effectively identified, monitored, and escalated? If not, then you'll need to tackle this gap head on. Otherwise, there's a real chance that all your work on business continuity is a waste. You won't invoke your plans at the right time, if at all.

2. Are incidents managed consistently across the organization? If not, then you'll need to bring some order either by standardizing processes or terminology or by having a mechanism that reconciles any discrepancies (i.e., one that recognizes that an incident IT may call a "critical I incident" is the same as what facilities call an "A status event").

3. Is there an effective command-and-control structure and supporting processes for dealing with disasters?

4. Where you have different business units in the same location, is the recovery of the location integrated? You may need to think about having an overarching plan that the crisis team will use to dictate the order of recovery for different functions.

5. Are all the key business lines included within your command-and-control structure? If not, then you'll need to make sure all business lines are represented in the command-and-control structure. If you have finance, IT, HR, and operations all in the same building, for example, they should all be represented at a management level, included in salient communications, and prioritized based on the immediate business need.

6. Do you have evacuation plans and marshaling points for all locations? If not, then you'll need to assess the need for marshaling points and decide on practical locations and embed this in your local processes.

7. Do you have trained marshals in all locations? If not, then you'll need to select and train marshals.

8. Does your staff know what to do if they get evacuated or can't get to work? If not, then you have a clear focus for your education and awareness initiatives.

9. Is your incident response set up to deal with incidents outside the traditional boundaries of your organization? In other words, would you be notified of a material supplier failure? If not, then you need to work with these suppliers to make sure your incident management processes integrate with theirs and that you are suitably notified of events.

Post Event

Return to Normal Operations

Getting your business back to "business as usual" can be a challenge. This chapter sets out what you need to do after you have invoked IT DR and how to minimize the risks. The approach also works for how to return to business as usual after invoking WAR.

Understanding the Different Planning Scenarios

There are a number of different scenarios that apply to a return to normal operations. They depend on the level of damage, the recovery architecture you've employed, and your attitude toward risk.

Production Is Still Intact

If you are lucky and the production site is intact, then reverting to production could be quite simple.

For systems, this is made simpler if you are able to replicate all new work completed in the DR location directly back to the normal production environment. Unfortunately, some DR designs only support replication in one direction. Consequently, you will need to reconfigure the DR environment to enable the recovery.

In many cases this is simply a matter of reversing the steps or even repeating the steps you originally took to invoke DR with some minor changes.

Production Is Without Replication or Is Unable to Return "Home"

If you have production but either don't have replication or it is not viable to return to the original production site or systems, then you are going to have to plan to get the latest data and software loaded back at the new production location, close down DR, and bring up production with all networks directing traffic to the right location.

This may mean copying data to tape, or it may mean physically applying software changes and reconfiguring computers and networks. The details can vary, but the need for manual intervention is guaranteed, along with the inherent risks. In the worst case, you will need to source a new site and hardware, which will not only engender significant risks but will also lead to lengthy delays.

Consider the Ongoing Risks

The post-DR risks to consider are:

- Loss of data

- Corruption of data

- Security breaches

- Extended outages if the switching from DR back to production overruns

You need to do a risk assessment as part of your plan to switch back, making sure that you cover each of these risks.

Take the Right Approach to Mitigate Risks

There are a variety of approaches to mitigate risks and get back to normal, which include the following:

- *Parallel running.* Get production and DR data synchronized and run both sites in parallel for a while until you are sure that it is okay to switch fully back. Parallel running can be done using batch processes to reprocess live transaction against the secondary site's databases.

- *Close down, start up.* This involves performing an orderly close down, normally at the end of the business day. You may complete all the normal batch work. Then restore the data in the target site before bringing the system up there.

- *New build.* You may have to build the systems, infrastructure, and data bases from scratch. This could be the result of having to find a new site, replacing hardware, or just the need to reintegrate changes that have been made since the system switched to run from the DR location. It can be very time-consuming and will involve extensive testing. There is significant risk of errors being made or issues emerging.

- *Lift and drop.* You may decide to physically take the equipment that is running in DR and ship it to the production site. This involves all the physical risks that are associated with the movement of equipment.

Planning the Return to Normal

Naturally, it will be easier to return to normal if you have planned for it in advance. In the majority of cases, the return-to-normal operations plan will be a reworking of the DR plan. Put simply, you take the plan for invoking DR and reverse it.

I recommend that you give this plenty of consideration when you are weighing your recovery strategy. Ask yourself, "How will we return to normal operations if either the production site is available again or the site is lost and a new site has to be sourced?" This is an important question that tests the viability of your options before you spend money developing it.

You should aim to adopt a strategy that lends itself to return to normal operations. This might sound obvious, but I can't tell you how often I've come across both WAR and DR solutions that would be almost impossible to revert— where the decision to invoke them in the first place is actually as painful as doing nothing.

As a basic outline, the plan should cover:

- How you going to revert operations. What are the alternatives? Why are you choosing this approach? This shouldn't be the length of *War and Peace,* but a brief overview to demonstrate the general rationale that has been applied.

- The specific actions you'll take.

- How you will test the action plan (both before and after the switch is completed).

- How you can stop the switch if you encounter issues. Identify any points of no return or major milestones where the mechanism for reverting the process changes.

- The risks and how you will manage them.

- How you will manage the process, escalate issues, and report progress.

- When the switch will be done. Again provide some rationale (e.g., bank holiday weekend as it provide some contingency time if issues are encountered).

- Who will approve the plan.

Once you have the plan, you need to get formal approval from the accountable managers. This will partly be dictated by your organization's change process and partly by who owns the overall risks and business services that are affected.

Tip If you can, work your WAR or DR plan such that returning to normal is simply reversing the steps in it. That will make your life much easier and the return less prone to glitches.

Maintaining Command and Control

Returning to normal operations is normally a time-critical and high-risk activity. It's not something I'd recommend delegating to data center operations or some other IT team.

You need to monitor progress closely and track any slippages to assess their overall potential to impact the recovery timescales. You'll also need to monitor any slippages and compare them with the possible reversion points. In particular, be aware of those for which you can't back out of the switch and bring production back up in DR without incurring an outage.

Depending on the risk and profile of the change, I recommend having management presence to oversee the switch and escalate any issues.

Action Plan

Reflect on the following questions and associated recommendations:

1. Do you know how you'll return to normal operations for each of the most likely scenarios? Is what you are planning actually the most sensible approach? Will it work? If not, then think about the strategies you'd employ using walkthroughs of your plans for the likely scenarios; assess the risks and include return-to-normal operations in your ongoing recovery testing.

2. Have you assessed the risks of having to return to normal operations? If not, then you'd better look at the options and assess the related risks.

3. Do you have a basic plan for returning to operations or could you just reverse the existing continuity plans? Think about what level of planning is appropriate and pull it together before it's too late.

Appendices

Criticality Levels

The following table is an example of criticality levels. The point is to determine when you absolutely must get an operation, process, or infrastructure back up and running, and then assign it a criticality level. If you're running a global finance operation, for example, you would probably need to assign payments processing a level of 0 or 1. HR systems, on the other hand, might rate a 4 or 5.

Only you know what makes sense for your company. You may decide to have more or have different descriptions or levels. It's the principle that matters; the exact implementation is irrelevant as long as it's consistent within your organization and represents a sensible way of breaking requirements up.

Level	Description of Criticality Level
0	Nonstop, continuous operation
1	Recovery within 2 hours
2	Recovery within 4 hours
3	Recovery within 12 hours
4	Recovery within 24 hours
5	Recovery within 48 hours
6	Recovery between 48 hours and 7 days
7	Recovery between 8 days and 1 month
8	Recovery not required. To be reviewed if interruption exceeds 4 weeks.

Roles and Responsibility Matrix

The following matrix—called RACI, which stands for Responsible, Accountable, Consulted, and Informed—sets out the high-level tasks that need to be undertaken in creating and sustaining a business continuity program. It's a very useful tool for making sure that the right things are planned with good engagement and communication.

It's not meant to be a flow chart, but it nevertheless provides a good basic tool with which to audit your program.

Key to Activity

Here's how each label is defined:

Responsible (R): The people, person, or team responsible for doing the activity.

Accountable (A): The person or body accountable for the activity being done. This includes making resources available, overseeing quality, and balancing the activity with other business priorities.

Consulted (C): The people, person, or team consulted as part of the process. These are the people who will help establish the who, what, why, where, when, and how of the activity.

Informed (I): The people, person, or team that is kept informed about the process.

Key to Roles

Here's what each of the roles mean:

Accountable manager: The manager who is accountable for the business operation under consideration—the person with the risk and budget!

Business continuity manager *(BCM):* The BCM normally manages the whole process and takes responsibility for some tasks.

Business recovery coordinator *(BRC):* The BRC is responsible for preparing and maintaining the business continuity plans.

Business staff: The ordinary members of staff who work within the function that are covered by business continuity.

IT service continuity managers (SCM: Those who coordinate the relationship with IT for everything that relates to continuity.

IT: The technical staff that supports disaster recovery (DR) and work area recovery (WAR)

Responsibilities	BCM	IT-SCM	IT	BRC	Business Staff	Accountable Manager
Set policy	R	C, I	C, I	C, I	I	A
Write strategy	R	C, I	C, I	C, I	I	A
Steering	R	C	C	C	C	R, A
Operating plan	A, R	C, I	C, I	C, I	C	I
RAID tracking (Risk Action Issues Decision Log)	R	C, I	C, I	C, I	C, I	A, C, I
Benchmarking	A, R	C, I	C, I	C, I	C	C, I
Waivers	R, I	R, I	R, I	R, I	C	A, C, I
Assertion	R	C	C	C, I	C	A, C, I
Trigger events	C, I	C, I	R	R, I	C	A
Business impact analysis	R	C, I	C, I	R	C, I	A, C, I
Risk assessment	C, I	C, I	C, I	R	C, I	A, C, I
Create workarounds	C, I	C, I	C, I	R	C, I	A, C, I
Complete business recovery plan	R	C, I	C, I	R	C, I	A, C, I
Complete data center recovery plan	C, I	R	R	C, I	I	A, C, I
Complete building plan	R	C, I	C, I	C, I	C, I	A, C, I

(continued)

Responsibilities	BCM	IT-SCM	IT	BRC	Business Staff	Accountable Manager
Complete crisis management plan	R	C, I	C, I	C, I	C, I	A, C, I
Desktop walkthroughs	R	C	C, I	R	C, I	A, C, I
Maintain battle boxes	R	C	C	R, A	C	C, I
Maintain contact lists	R	C	C	R, A	C	C, I
Maintain test schedule	A, R	C, I	C, I	C, I	C, I	I
Disaster recovery test	C	R	A, R	C, I	C, I	I
Work area recovery test	R	R	C, I	C, I	C, I	A, I
Crisis management exercise	R	C, I	C, I	C, I	C, I	A, C, I
Complete call cascade	R	C	C, I	A, R	C, I	C, I
Education and awareness	A, R	C, I	C, I	C, I	I	I
Third-party reviews	A, R	R	C, I	R	I	I
Third-party testing	A, R	R	R	R	I	I

Suggested Business Continuity Management Timetable

Use this timetable to plan events, remind yourself of what needs to be done, and stay on top of your continuity responsibilities.

When	What	Who
Ad hoc/annually	Plan reviews: Besides the annual review, these should be done when a trigger event occurs, such as after a major change, new products, and so forth.	Business unit managers, business continuity manager
Annually/ad hoc	Business impact analysis (BIA)	Business unit managers, business continuity manager

(continued)

When	What	Who
Annually	Plan walkthrough	Business unit managers, business continuity manager
Semiannually	Call cascade review	Business unit managers, business continuity manager
Annually	Work area recovery (WAR) test	Business unit managers, business continuity manager, IT
Annually	IT disaster recovery (DR) test	Business unit manager, business continuity manager, IT
Annually	Crisis management exercise	Crisis management team, business continuity manager
Annually	Staff awareness events and training	Business continuity manager
Annually	Executive briefings	Business continuity manager

Useful Resources and Contacts

This list includes useful contact information on business continuity organizations, regulatory and legal information, industry resources, planning, and guidance. It will be helpful to anyone in business continuity and disaster recovery positions, but especially for those new to the discipline.

Business Continuity Organizations

Association of Contingency Planners (www.acp-international.com)

Business Continuity Institute (www.thebci.org)

Business Continuity Management Institute (www.bcm-institute.org)

Business Resilience Certification Consortium International (BRCCI) (www.brcci.org)

The Institute for Continuity Management/DRI International (www.drii.org)

Business Continuity Standards

17799 Central (www.17799central.com)

American Standards Institute (ANSI) (www.ansi.org)

Australian/New Zealand Standard (AUS/NZ) (www.standards.org.au)

British Standards Institution (BSI) (www.bsi-global.com)

International Organization of Standards (ISO) (www.iso.org)

ISO 17799 Newsletter (http://17799-news.the-hamster.com)

National, Regional, Government, and Law

Canadian Centre for Emergency (CCEP) Preparedness (www.ccep.ca)

Department of Homeland Security Emergency Plan Guidelines (www.ready.gov/business/index.html)

Federal Emergency Management Agency (www.fema.gov)

Foreign & Commonwealth Office (www.fco.gov.uk)

Home Office (www.homeoffice.gov.uk)

London Prepared (www.londonprepared.gov.uk/businesscontinuity)

MI5 (www.mi5.gov.uk)

NISCC: National Infrastructure Security Co-ordination Centre (www.cpni.gov.uk)

UK Emergency Response and Recovery Resilience (www.gov.uk/emergency-response-and-recovery)

Financial Services and Insurance

Association of British Insurers (www.abi.org.uk)

Australian Securities and Investments Commission (www.asic.gov.au/asic/asic.nsf)

Australian Prudential Regulation Authority (APRA) I Standard APS232: Business Continuity Management (www.apra.gov.au)

Federal Financial Institutions Examination Council's Information Technology Examination Handbook (FFIEC) (http://ithandbook.ffiec.gov/)

Financial Sector Continuity (www.fsc.gov.uk)

Financial Services Authority (www.fsa.gov.uk)

Emergency Planning

Emergency Planning Society (www.the-eps.org)

Emergency Planning College (www.epcollege.com/epc/home/)

Fire and Flood

Environment Agency (www.environment-agency.gov.uk)

FEMA Flood Information (www.ready.gov/floods)

London Fire Brigade (www.london-fire.gov.uk/)

National Fire Protection Association (www.nfpa.org/)

UK Fire Service (www.fireservice.co.uk/safety)

UK Flood Line (free hotline from the Environment Agency):
+44 (0) 845-988-1188

Publications, Websites, White Papers, and Guidance

A Disaster Recovery Plan: National Library of Australia (www.nla.gov.au/policy/disaster)

AT&T Business Continuity Study 2008 (US) (www.att.com/gen/pressroom?pid=7922)

Cabinet Office Study into BCM (www.managers.org.uk/research-analysis/research/current-research/decade-living-dangerously-business-continuity-management)

CIDRAP/SHRM Pandemic HR Guide Toolkit (www.cidrap.umn.edu/cidrap/files/33/cidrap-shrm-hr-pandemic-toolkit.pdf)

Continuity Central (www.continuitycentral.com)

Continuity Central 2006 Global Survey (www.continuitycentral.com/feature0358.htm)

Continuity Forum (www.continuityforum.org)

Continuity Insurance & Risk (formerly Corporate Insurance & Risk) (www.cirmagazine.com/cir/index.php)

Disaster Recovery Information Exchange (DRIE) (www.drie.org/index.php)

Disaster Recover Journal (www.drj.com)

Disaster Recovery Planning—Project Plan Outline—University of Toronto (www.utoronto.ca/security/documentation/business_continuity/dis_rec_plan.htm)

Disaster Resource.com (www.disaster-resource.com)

Gartner—The Aftermath: Disaster Recovery and Planning for the Future (www.gartner.com/5_about/news/disaster_recovery.html)

Glossary of Business Continuity Terms (www.bcmpedia.org)

Incorporating Pandemic Risk into an Advanced Measurement Approach for Operational Risk Management, May 2009 (www.complispace.com.au/Assets/411/1/pandemicrisk.pdf)

London First Secure in the Knowledge (www.londonfirst.co.uk/documents/097_Secure_in_the_Knowledge.pdf)

London First Expecting the Unexpected (www.londonfirst.co.uk/documents/117_Expecting_the_Unexpected.pdf)

Continuity Assessment Questionnaire

This questionnaire will help you get an understanding of your strengths and weaknesses regarding business continuity. For more background on the assessment, how to score it, and the meaning of "tier," see the "Where Do You Stand Today?" section of Chapter 2.

Element	Controls	Output	Tier	Score	Maturity	Target Maturity	Target Score
Governance	Is there a BCM policy that's documented, maintained, and signed off on by senior management?	Policy	I				
Governance	Is there a suitable steering committee that meets regularly and is attended by the necessary quorum of members?	Steering committee	I				
Governance	Is there a simple reporting pack or set of KPIs that identifies things that need management intervention?	KPI/ reporting pack	I				
Governance	Have you documented your BCM lifecycle and the supporting management system? Do you have a set of standards against which performance and maturity can be assessed?	Standards	2				
Governance	Is there a documented strategy that explains how the policy will be met? Is the strategy reviewed and updated at the same time as the policy or when there are major changes in the business?	Strategy	2				
Governance	Has the organization's risk appetite been agreed to by the steering committee and is it documented?	Risk appetite	2				
Governance	Are all the activities that make up the ongoing business continuity program budgeted, planned, and resourced?	Operating plan	2				

(continued)

Element	Controls	Output	Tier	Score	Maturity	Target Maturity	Target Score
Governance	Are any improvement initiatives documented, planned, budgeted, and resourced or has a waiver or exemption certificate been agreed upon?	Remediation program	2				
Governance	Are all BCM risks, issues, actions, and key decisions recorded in a central log? Are all items owned by someone with due dates?	RAID (Risk, Action, Issues, and Decisions log) tracking	2				
Governance	Are BCM competencies assessed against regulatory and industry best practices, with target maturity levels set?	Maturity assessment	2				
Governance	Has a report on BCM been made to the organization's board and recorded in board minutes?	Management report	3				
Governance	Are all repeatable activities documented to a level where someone who is unfamiliar with the activity could perform it efficiently and effectively?	Work instructions	3				
Governance	Do any exceptions to policy or standards have a waiver or exemption certificate? Are all waivers reviewed annually?	Waiver process	3				
Governance	Has management asserted that their BIA is a true reflection of their business needs and that their BCPs meet their needs? Are proven strategies in place to ensure smooth recovery?	Assertion Process	3				

(continued)

Element	Controls	Output	Tier	Score	Maturity	Target Maturity	Target Score
Governance	Do business changes trigger a review of the business continuity provisions?	Trigger process	3				
Understand the Business	Is the BIA completed within agreed timescales and formally signed off by management? Does the BIA assess business criticality from a legal, regulatory, financial, reputational, and customer perspective? Are all critical resources identified including people, systems, infrastructure, and facilities? Is a recovery profile created that sets out the recovery of resources and tasks over time? Are all critical dependencies identified? Are all gaps reported to management for review and remediation?	BIA	1				
Understand the Business	Is a risk assessment completed for key locations and business areas? Is the risk assessment reviewed when BCM strategies are being selected or reviewed?	Risk Assessment	1				
Capability	Do all systems have a recovery time objective (RTO), last test time (actual RTO), and IT SLA (the RTO that IT actually signs off on) documented?	Global systems status tracking	1				
Capability	Do DR solutions meet business requirements?	DR solutions	2				
Capability	Do WAR solutions meet business requirements?	WAR solution	2				
Capability	Are all gaps in DR and WAR documented? Are agreed-upon gaps included in the remediation plan?	DR remediation plan	2				

(continued)

Element	Controls	Output	Tier	Score	Maturity	Target Maturity	Target Score
Capability	Has the resilience of critical systems and processes been assessed? Are gaps identified for review by management?	Resilience	2				
Capability	Have workarounds been identified and documented for all critical processes and resources that need them?	Workaround instructions	2				
Capability	Are IT architectural standards documented and agreed upon? Do they map criticality, levels of service, and corresponding architecture guidelines?	Architectural standards	3				
Planning	Is a simple BCP template available that includes an action plan, contacts details, call cascades, useful numbers, escalation process, and directions to all recovery facilities?	BCP templates	1				
Planning	Do all departments have a suitable person and an alternate to ensure that the business continuity plan is prepared and maintained in line with the guidance set forth in the standards?	Business continuity coordinators appointed	1				
Planning	Does every data center have a plan that documents the closedown and recovery of the environment, infrastructure, and services? Does the plan cater to the likely scenarios (e.g., orderly closedown, intraday failure, prebatch, postbatch, intrabatch, etc.)?	Data center recovery plans	1				

(continued)

Element	Controls	Output	Tier	Score	Maturity	Target Maturity	Target Score
Planning	Does each system or IT service have a recovery plan that details the exact steps required to recover the system? Is the plan written at a level that a competent professional could recover the service?	System/service recovery plans	2				
Planning	Do building level recovery plans exist? Do they set out how all the different areas within a building will be recovered?	Building recovery plans	2				
Planning	Are lists of critical contacts maintained?	Contacts	2				
Planning	Have all critical activities been identified? Have resource bottlenecks and single points of failure been identified?	Critical processes	2				
Planning	Are materials, manual workarounds, and other working instructions stored at the recovery center or can they be delivered there within the RTO? Are battle box contents reviewed as directed in the standard?	Battle boxes	3				
Testing	Is a rolling test plan maintained that details all test activity?	Test schedule	2				
Testing	Does every test follow a test plan that sets out the test objectives, approach, success criteria, metrics, resources, activities, and budget? Does the test plan include a detailed test script that is followed throughout the test and reported against at the end?	Test plans	2				

(continued)

Element	Controls	Output	Tier	Score	Maturity	Target Maturity	Target Score
Testing	Are posttest meetings completed within the timescales set out in the standard? Are all risks, issues, and lessons reviewed and actions agreed upon, planned, and owned?	Posttest meetings	2				
Testing	Is a test report produced within the timescales set out in the BCM standards? Does the report cover the test approach, an assessment of the extent to which test objectives were met, timings, issues, and action plan? Is the test report approved by management?	Test reports	2				
Testing	Is every system tested as per the standards for the level of criticality? Are all issues captured and reported to management for review and remediation?	DR unit test	2				
Testing	Has every team with a business recovery requirement participated in a denial of access test? Are issues captured and reported to management for review and remediation?	DOA testing	2				
Testing	Is a walkthrough of the data center recovery plan undertaken with all the key role holders?	Data center recovery plan walkthrough	2				

(continued)

Element	Controls	Output	Tier	Score	Maturity	Target Maturity	Target Score
Testing	Are all business recovery plans subjected to desktop walkthroughs where the business recovery team is brought together to complete a desktop scenario? Is the session independently facilitated and are all actions captured and reported to senior management for review and remediation?	Desktop plan walkthrough	2				
Testing	Do all teams complete a regular call notification cascade test? Is the cascade independently facilitated? Are timings, success or failure, and all actions captured and reported to management for review and remediation? If required, are additional building, enterprise, and crisis management team cascades conducted?	Cascade tests	2				
Testing	Are key products and services subjected to end-to-end testing?	End-to-end tests	3				
Testing	Has full data center recovery been tested demonstrating that all systems can be recovered within the required timescales? Are all people with a role in data center recovery obliged to take part in a data center test as standards require?	Data center recovery test	3				
Testing	Do test scripts exist that detail the exact steps to be taken including any data entry, system responses, or contacts?	Test scripts	3				

(continued)

Element	Controls	Output	Tier	Score	Maturity	Target Maturity	Target Score
Crisis management	Is the crisis management plan updated frequently enough and after significant changes? Does those who use the plan have a copy of the latest plan and have all old versions been destroyed?	Crisis management plan	2				
Crisis management	Are crisis management exercises conducted with adequate frequency? Do all members and their deputies partake in the exercises?	CM exercise	2				
Crisis response	Does the framework exist that sets out how business incidents should be reported, monitored, and escalated to crisis management? Is the framework resilient and have no single points of failure? Is media independent handover (MIH) tested regularly and issues documented, owned, and, where necessary, actions planned?	MIH framework	1				
Crisis response	Have all business lines and IT teams adopted the MIH framework and process?	MIH rollout	3				
Education and awareness (E&A)	Have all business continuity coordinators and their deputies been briefed on their roles and responsibilities?	Business continuity coordinator training	1				
E&A	Have all members of the crisis management team and their deputies been briefed on their roles and responsibilities?	Crisis management team training	1				

(continued)

Element	Controls	Output	Tier	Score	Maturity	Target Maturity	Target Score
E&A	Do all new joiners receive some training on business continuity? Are they made aware of what to expect if the most likely scenarios occurred and what they should do?	Induction training	2				
E&A	Has everyone with a recovery role, as part of business continuity plans or IT DR plans, been briefed on their roles and responsibilities, and have they taken part in an exercise?	Business recovery team training	2				
E&A	Has everyone who conducts a BIA been trained in the BIA process, tool, analysis, and supporting templates?	BIA training	2				
E&A	Has everyone who maintains business recovery plans been trained in plan creation and maintenance?	BRP training	2				
E&A	Are all senior managers briefed on their business continuity plan? Are they aware of any gaps or issues?	Senior management briefings	2				
E&A	Do all staff have essential contact information on hand (e.g., on back of staff pass, in a wallet card, etc.)?	Emergency contact information	2				
E&A	Are accurate training records maintained for everyone who has a business continuity role? Does the record track key competences, roles, and responsibilities?	Training tracker	3				

(continued)

Element	Controls	Output	Tier	Score	Maturity	Target Maturity	Target Score
E&A	Have events and activities been identified and planned that will raise awareness of business continuity and make all staff aware of what to expect and what to do if the most key scenarios occurred?	Awareness program	3				
E&A	Has every member of staff been briefed by their manager on the contents of their business continuity plan, what to expect if the key scenarios occur, and what they should do?	All staff BCM briefings	3				
Third party	Are all third parties identified and ranked in terms of their criticality? Are those deemed as critical prioritized and assessed first? Does assessment identify recovery requirements, actual capability, and business dependencies?	Third-party assessment	2				
Third party	Are dependent functions recorded along with the associated recovery requirements?	Third-party reporting	2				
Third party	Have standard terms and conditions been defined for insertion into contracts? Is business continuity integrated into the procurement process and included as a requirement in all new arrangements?	Contract terms and conditions	2				
Third party	Do third parties undertake testing that demonstrates the required recovery capability? Do they have records of tests including test plans, scripts, and reports available for review if required?	Third-party testing	2				

Element	Controls	Output	Tier	Score	Maturity	Target Maturity	Target Score
Third party	Do critical third parties have the process and capability in place to notify management of any incident that threatens or impairs the delivery of their goods or services?	Third-party notification	3				
BCM function	Are all roles and their corresponding responsibilities documented with clear demarcation of responsibility and accountability?	RACI	2				
BCM function	Do staff information lines exists with access controls in place that restricts updating of the line to nominated members of staff? Are all staff aware of the number? Is access and maintenance tested regularly?	Staff information line	3				
BCM function	Is the business continuity team structure, including virtual (matrix) resources, reviewed regularly to ensure that there are enough resources and they are organized to support the ongoing business continuity program?	Organizational design for BCM	3				

Crisis Management Team Roles and Responsibilities

This list can be used to pinpoint responsibilities in a crisis.

Role	Responsibility
Crisis leader	• Assess incidents and decide if the crisis team should convene and who should be involved.
	• Chair crisis management team sessions.
	• Oversee the management of all risks and issues and ensure that adequate action is planned and adequate progress is being made.
	• Escalate issues where the crisis leadership team lacks authority or is failing to make adequate progress.
	• Approve crisis management team decisions.
	• Ensure crisis management process is being followed by all members.

(continued)

Role	Responsibility
	• Provide crisis management team with clear direction and support.
	• Ensure that adequate resources are being made available.
	• Undertake key communication with media, staff, customers, and major stakeholders.
Business continuity manager	• Advise crisis leader on invocation of the crisis management team and its constituents.
	• Advise crisis management team of appropriate processes and actions.
	• Coordinate the execution of business recovery plans.
	• Provide a crisis command center and ensure that it is suitably equipped.
	• Oversee crisis leadership call cascades to notify members of the situation and any meetings that are required.
Support	• Provide administrative support to the crisis management team.
	• Maintain command center records of events (e.g., key events, issues, risks, and actions, etc.) using whiteboards and event, issue, risk, and action logs.
	• Collate incoming intelligence and present salient facts for the crisis management team to review.
Emergency services liaison	• Ensure that there is an ongoing good relationship with the local emergency services and that your processes align with theirs.
	• Initiate contact with emergency services in times of crisis.
	• Assess incoming information, identifying salient news, risks, issues, and actions.
	• Escalate risks, issues, and actions that exceed the liaison's authority or directly impact others to the crisis leader for review and authorization.
	• Provide the crisis management team with a summary of salient facts.
Facilities	• Ensure that facilities are secured and that building services and infrastructure are in place.
	• Assess the information being passed from the facilities team, identifying salient news, risks, issues, and actions.
	• Escalate risks, issues, and actions that exceed the facilities members' authority or directly impact other areas to the crisis leader for review and authorization.

(continued)

Role	Responsibility
	• Lead the recovery of any facilities teams impacted by the crisis, giving the facilities recovery team direction, monitoring progress or escalating issues, and providing timely feedback.
	• Make tactical decisions about how critical facilities and related services will be provided throughout any period of disruption.
	• Provide the crisis management team a summary of salient facts as they relate to facilities and security.
	• Provide members of the crisis management team support and direction on any matters relating to HR.
Communications	• Ensure that critical business communications continue with minimum disruption throughout any times of crisis.
	• Ensure that communications staff have the resources and facilities they need to complete their responsibilities.
	• Assess the information being passed from the communications team, identifying salient news, risks, issues, and actions.
	• Escalate risks, issues, and actions that exceed the communications crisis team member's authority or directly impact other areas to the crisis leader for review and authorization.
	• Lead the recovery of any communications teams impacted by the crisis, giving the communications recovery team direction, monitoring progress or escalating issues, and providing timely feedback.
	• Make tactical decisions about how information will be provided throughout any period of disruption.
	• Ensure that all inquiries from the media are handled professionally.
	• Provide the crisis management team a summary of salient facts as they relate to communication.
	• Provide members of the crisis management team support and direction on any matters relating to communication.
HR	• Ensure that staff welfare is maintained throughout any times of crisis.
	• Ensure that staff and their families receive accurate information and, where appropriate, counseling is provided.
	• Assess the information being passed from the HR team, identifying salient news, risks, issues, and actions.

(continued)

Role	Responsibility
	• Escalate risks, issues, and actions that exceed the HR member's authority or directly impact other areas to the crisis leader for review and authorization.
	• Lead the recovery of any HR teams impacted by the crisis, giving the HR recovery team direction, monitoring progress or escalating issues, and providing timely feedback.
	• Make tactical decisions about how critical HR services will be provided throughout any period of disruption.
	• Provide the crisis management team a summary of salient facts as they relate to HR.
	• Provide members of the crisis management team support and direction on any matters relating to HR.
IT	• Ensure that critical IT services are maintained with minimum disruption throughout any times of crisis.
	• Ensure that the business gets the technical support it needs in order to expedite the rapid recovery of the business and its infrastructure.
	• Ensure that IT staff have the resources and facilities they need to complete their responsibilities.
	• Assess the information being passed from the IT team, identifying salient news, risks, issues, and actions.
	• Escalate risks, issues, and actions that exceed the IT crisis team member's authority or directly impact other areas to the crisis leader for review and authorization.
	• Lead the recovery of critical IT services impacted by the crisis.
	• Lead the recovery of any IT teams impacted by the crisis, giving the IT recovery team direction, monitoring progress or escalating issues, and providing timely feedback.
	• Make tactical decisions about how critical IT services will be provided throughout any period of disruption.
	• Provide the crisis management team a summary of salient facts as they relate to IT.
	• Provide members of the crisis management team support and direction on any matters relating to IT.

(continued)

Role	Responsibility
Business heads	• Ensure that critical business activities continue with minimum disruption throughout any times of crisis. • Ensure that their staff have the resources and facilities they need to complete their responsibilities. • Assess the information being passed from their teams, identifying salient news, risks, issues, and actions. • Escalate risks, issues, and actions that exceed their authority or directly impact other areas to the crisis leader for review and authorization. • Lead the recovery of any of their teams impacted by the crisis, giving the communications recovery team direction, monitoring progress or escalating issues, and providing timely feedback. • Provide the crisis management team a summary of salient facts as they relate to communication. • Provide members of the crisis management team support and direction on any matters relating to their line of business.

Call Cascade

Chapter 2 discusses call cascades and how they work. This is a template you can adapt to your situation.

Primary Contact

Name:

Home:

Mobile:

Office:

Other:

E-mail:

Alternate

Name:

Home:

Mobile:

Office:

Other:

E-mail:

The primary contact or their alternate calls each of the cascade leads or their alternates. The leads then call their groups, and each of them calls their groups, etc.

Cascade 1	Cascade 2	Cascade 3
Name:	Name:	Name:
Home:	Home:	Home:
Mobile:	Mobile:	Mobile:
Office:	Office:	Office:
Other:	Other:	Other:
E-mail:	E-mail:	E-mail:
Name:	Name:	Name:
Home:	Home:	Home:
Mobile:	Mobile:	Mobile:
Office:	Office:	Office:
Other:	Other:	Other:
E-mail:	E-mail:	E-mail:
Name:	Name:	Name:
Home:	Home:	Home:
Mobile:	Mobile:	Mobile:
Office:	Office:	Office:
Other:	Other:	Other:
E-mail:	E-mail:	E-mail:
Name:	Name:	Name:
Home:	Home:	Home:
Mobile:	Mobile:	Mobile:
Office:	Office:	Office:
Other:	Other:	Other:
E-mail:	E-mail:	E-mail:
Name:	Name:	Name:
Home:	Home:	Home:
Mobile:	Mobile:	Mobile:
Office:	Office:	Office:
Other:	Other:	Other:
E-mail:	E-mail:	E-mail:

Basic Business Continuity Plan Template

As mentioned in Chapter 4, the business continuity plan (BCP) details what you'll need to do to keep your business running or get it back up and running in a disaster or significant problem. It details specific actions, and it contains all the contact details and other essential information that will get you through the first few hours of a problem and then beyond it.

Business Continuity Plan

Business unit name	Name of business area	**Location**	The location covered by the plan
Plan author	Person responsible for creating the plan	**Plan approver**	The person accountable for the business area's plan
BCM manager	Point of contact in the business continuity management team	**Business recovery coordinator**	The person who maintains the plans and liaises with the BCM team
Last updated	Date that the plan was last updated	**Review due**	The date by when the plan must be reviewed
Approved by	The person who last approved the plan	**Approval date**	The date on which the plan was last formally approved

Plan Change Record			
Version/Date	**Change**	**Name**	**Status**
1.0/April 2014	Create draft plan	Jamie Watters	Open

Key Contacts

Role	Name	Home	Mobile	Other
What do they do?	*Full name*	*Home telephone number*	*Mobile telephone number*	*Any other contact information (e.g., e-mail addresses, second home, Blackberry, etc.)*
Crisis leader				
IT				
HR				
Facilities				
PR/communications				
Administrative assistant				
Business unit leader 1				
Business unit leader 2				
Business unit leader 3				
Add contacts as required				

Useful Numbers

Resource	Number	Resource	Number
Crisis conference line		Staff information line	
Security		Head office	
IT operations		IT help desk	
DR provider		WAR provider	
Supplier 1		Supplier 2	
Add contacts as required			

Escalation Process

On identifying an incident or the potential for one, the initial responders should escalate to the BCM manager, who will monitor the incident and escalate to the crisis leader, who, with the business continuity manager, will decide if the crisis management team needs to be convened.

RESPONDER

BUSINESS CONTINUITY MANAGER

CRISIS LEADER

CRISIS MANAGEMENT TEAM

CEO/BOARD

The crisis management team will assess the situation and adjust the exact recovery order based on events, opportunities, and current business priorities. Where they are unable to execute plans or require a decision that exceeds their authority, then the crisis leader will escalate to the board.

Initial Response Checklist

What must you do first? Add items as necessary.

#	Action	Done✓
1.	Identify the current situation and any impacts on:	
	• Staff	
	• Customers	
	• Facilities	
	• Technology	
	• Suppliers	
	• Revenue	
2.	Establish what actions are being taken, what the likely resolution is, and when this will be achieved	
3.	Start an incident log	
4.	Assess if the crisis management team needs to convene and who should be involved	
5.	Set the time and place for the first crisis meeting	
6.	Initiate call cascade	
7.	Determine if any additional actions are required before the crisis management team convenes	
8.	Invoke recovery plans as required by situation	

Day 0 Action Plan

This section details what happens the moment a crisis occurs.

#	Action	Done✓
1.	Switch inbound calls to other offices; direct as many callers as possible to the Internet site	
2.	Ensure all accounts are settled	
3.	Prepare message for customers, suppliers, etc.	
4.	Insert place-holding message on Internet site	
5.	Deploy manual workarounds if IT systems are unavailable	
6.	Notify key accounts and suppliers of situation, make recommendations, and advise that you will update them via e-mail	
7.	As soon as customer service staff are available, start working on priority customer accounts	

(continued)

#	Action	Done✓
8.	As customer service staff increases, take more incoming calls and focus on priority calls, asking nonurgent customers to call back or direct them to the Internet	
9.	Reassess situation and update communications, making sure that key clients, suppliers, and the web site are updated	
10.	Prepare Day 1 plan	
11.	Mobilize Day 1 resources	

Critical Activities List

Critical activities will of course vary from business to business. For example, if you're in the grocery business and your freezers fail, you need to move the goods fast—with an RTO of maybe an hour or less. An information-based business would have an entirely different set of priorities.

Critical Activity	When It Must Be Recovered (RTO)	Done✓
Service customer queries	24 hours	
Outbound sales call	1 week	
(Add all critical activities and RTOs)		

Critical Systems List

Critical systems are those you can't do business without. They will vary from organization to organization and industry to industry. You will no doubt have some that must be back up and running within hours to ensure your business doesn't experience a catastrophe.

Critical Systems	When It Must Be Recovered (RTO)	Done✓
Internet site	1 hour	
Telephones	4 hours	
Customer database	24 hours	
HR	48 hours	
(Add more critical systems and RTOs)		

Work Transfer List

This part of the plan details how you will transfer critical activities to alternate sites or third parties.

Critical Activity	Where to	Done✓
Switch in bound calls to other contact centers.	Newcastle, Bangalore, Kuala Lumpur	
Customer transactions	Internet site	
(Add more actions as necessary)		

Recovery Profile

This template can be used to assign people to a WAR desk both so people know where to go but also so support people in IT and other capacities can outfit the workspace appropriately.

Desk	Name	Role	Alternate	Day
Example	Fred Blogs	Manager	John Smith	0 (or 1, 2, 3, etc.)
1				
2				
3				
4				
5				

Additional Equipment List

This is simply about what equipment you need and when. Again, it's highly situational.

Resource	When It Must Be Recovered (RTO)	Done✓
Fax	4 hour	
Printer	4 hours	
(Add more equipment as necessary)		

Call Cascade

There is a more comprehensive call cascade template in Appendix G.

Primary Contact

Name:

Home:

Mobile:

Office:

Other:

Email:

Alternate

Name:

Home:

Mobile:

Office:

Other:

E-mail:

The primary contact or their alternate calls each of the cascade leads or their alternates, each of whom then calls another set of people, and so on.

Cascade 1	Cascade 2	Cascade 3
Name:	Name:	Name:
Home:	Home:	Home:
Mobile:	Mobile:	Mobile:
Office:	Office:	Office:
Other:	Other:	Other:
E-mail:	E-mail:	E-mail:

(continued)

Cascade 1	Cascade 2	Cascade 3
Name:	Name:	Name:
Home:	Home:	Home:
Mobile:	Mobile:	Mobile:
Office:	Office:	Office:
Other:	Other:	Other:
E-mail:	E-mail:	E-mail:
Name:	Name:	Name:
Home:	Home:	Home:
Mobile:	Mobile:	Mobile:
Office:	Office:	Office:
Other:	Other:	Other:
E-mail:	E-mail:	E-mail:
Name:	Name:	Name:
Home:	Home:	Home:
Mobile:	Mobile:	Mobile:
Office:	Office:	Office:
Other:	Other:	Other:
E-mail:	E-mail:	E-mail:
Name:	Name:	Name:
Home:	Home:	Home:
Mobile:	Mobile:	Mobile:
Office:	Office:	Office:
Other:	Other:	Other:
E-mail:	E-mail:	E-mail:

(continued)

Cascade 1	Cascade 2	Cascade 3
Name:	Name:	Name:
Home:	Home:	Home:
Mobile:	Mobile:	Mobile:
Office:	Office:	Office:
Other:	Other:	Other:
E-mail:	E-mail:	E-mail:

Contingency Site Details

Address of site:

Contact names and details:

Directions to the contingency site:

Travel arrangements for getting to the site via rail, bus, etc.:

Map of contingency site locations:

Map showing the route from place of work to the contingency site:

Useful information like local hotels, restaurants, etc.:

Assembly Point Details

Exact positions of assembly points (include maps if possible and directions if necessary):

.

Business Impact Analysis Questionnaire

The BIA questionnaire is part of the BIA process, which establishes what is critical to business survival and how that will translate into recovery priorities or requirements. Chapter 3 describes more on the process. Note that this is a "short-form" version of a BIA questionnaire.

1. General Information

Function name:

Analyst's name:

Job title:

Mobile telephone number:

Home telephone number:

Alternate telephone number:

E-mail address:

Function description:

For the purposes of this BIA, we have defined a "significant" impact as:

- The potential loss of $1 million in profits
- Fines or compensation in excess of $500,000
- A private warning from a lead regulator
- A serious breach of industry rules
- A prominent negative article in a leading media outlet
- The potential permanent loss of one or more high-profile clients
- Litigation resulting in loss of reputation, fines, or lengthy legal proceedings

---

■ **Note** You will need to establish your own criteria for a significant impact. It's probable that you will need to set much lower thresholds for potential loss and introduce some totally new aspects that are unique or relevant to your industry.

---

2. Critical Activities

List your function's activities or processes. When listing the functions, think about when would be the worst possible time in the business cycle (e.g., volatile markets, end of accounting period, one hour before a specific deadline, etc.) for a disruption to normal operations. Assuming a disruption at the worst possible time in the business cycle, how long would it be before the "significant" impact threshold is breached? If you need to, add more functions add rows as required.

ID	Key Activities or Processes	Worst Time for Disruption	Time to Breach Threshold
1.			
2.			
3.			
4.			
5.			

3. Internal Dependencies

For each of your activities or processes, are there any upstream activities or processes on which you depend? There may be more than one for any of them. If the upstream activity or process was disrupted, how long would it be before your activity or process experienced a "significant" disruption?

ID	Key Activities or Processes	Upstream Activities or Processes	Amount of Time to Disrupt My Activity or Process
1.			
2.			
3.			
4.			
5.			

4. External Dependencies

For each of your activities or process, are there external suppliers on which you depend? There may be more than one for any of your activities or processes. If the external supplier was disrupted, how long would it be before your activity or process experienced "significant" disruption?

ID	Key Activities or Processes	Supplier	Amount of Time to Disrupt My Activity or Process
1.			
2.			
3.			
4.			
5.			

5. Systems Dependencies

Identify any systems used to deliver each of your activities or processes. List systems each time they are needed if they are used to support different activities or processes. Assuming a system's disruption at the worst possible time in the business cycle, how long would it be before the "significant" impact threshold is breached? Likewise, working back from the point in time when the outage occurred, how much data could you afford to lose? In other words, how much time could you leave between backups of the data? To answer this, think about how you would rekey information, if this were possible. Make allowances for the viability of rekeying data if you are operating in recovery and think about the point in time when any backlog would become overwhelming.

ID	Key Activities or Processes	Systems Used	Time to Breach Threshold	Data Loss (RPO)
1.				
2.				
3.				
4.				
5.				

6. Manual Workarounds

Identify any manual workarounds that could be used to delay the breach of the "significant" impact threshold and how long they could be used before catching up would be close to impossible. What strategies could you employ while you wait for your systems, people, or processes to be restored? A good example might be to switch all inbound calls to another office and stop all outbound calls until the recovery is completed.

ID	Key Activities or Processes	Workaround	Length of Workaround
1.			
2.			
3.			
4.			
5.			

7. Work Transfer

Identify whether any of your activities or processes could be carried out by staff in another office or by a third party. Identify any barriers to transferring this activity or process that might exist (e.g., systems access, training, criticality of existing workload, etc.).

ID	Key Activities or rocesses	Alternate Office	Barriers to Transfer
1.			
2.			
3.			
4.			
5.			

8. Desktop Profile

Thinking of the function as a whole, what are your minimum IT requirements at a recovery site over each of the following timeframes? These requirements are to ensure that no activity or process breaches the "significant" threshold in the event of a disruption. For each desk (e.g., 1–12), indicate the requirement using the following scale:

    I - Immediate

    S - Same day

    N - Next day

    F - Following Monday

Add additional rows to the table as required. If you require more than 12 desks, you can copy and paste the table.

Next, identify applications required and in what timeframe. Note that a standard desktop includes Outlook, MS Office, and a telephone handset.

Desk No.:	1.	2.	3.	4.	5.	6.	7.	8.	9.	10.	11.	12.
Requirement												
Example: Standard desktop	I	N	N	I	S	I	I	F	S	S	I	F
Standard desktop												
Application 1												
Application 2												
Application 3												
Application 4												
Application 5												

(continued)

Desk No.:	1.	2.	3.	4.	5.	6.	7.	8.	9.	10.	11.	12.
Requirement												
Market data 1												
Market data 2												

9. Staff Recovery Profile

Thinking of the function as a whole, what is the total number of staff allocated to the process or activity to support business-as-usual operation? In order to ensure that no activity or process breaches the "significant" threshold in the event of a disruption, what are your minimum staff levels at a recovery site over each of the following timeframes?

> I - Immediate
>
> S - Same day
>
> N - Next day
>
> F - Following Monday

How long would this be sustainable (i.e., how long before you would need to revert to business-as-usual staffing levels)?

Next, note the key activities in your function. Please add additional rows to the table as required.

Key Activity or Process:	Total Staff	I	S	N	F	How Many Days Until You Must Return to Full Capacity
Example: Sales	16	0	4	4	8	28
Activity 1						
Activity 2						
Activity 3						
Activity 4						
Activity 5						

10. Recovery Strategy

In the event of a disruption, explain your preferred strategy (e.g., manage risk, suspend sales to focus on customer service, etc.) and how it might change over time. Note that relocating to a recovery site or working from home is not a strategy in itself but the method for achieving the strategy.

My preferred strategy:

11. Additional Requirements

Are there any extra requirements to enable the desired recovery strategy?

How quickly are these needed?

      I - Immediate

      S - Same day

      N - Next day

      F - Following Monday

Please add additional rows to the table as required.

Requirements:	Number of Staff	I	S	N	F	How Many Days Until You Must Return to Full Capacity
Example: Scanner	0	0	I	I	I	28
Example: Truck	3	0	I	2	I	14

Business Continuity Management Standards

As mentioned in Chapter 1, standards have been devised to help organizations perform important activities in a consistent and high-quality way. They also help different organizations work together. There are country and international standards, both governed by a group of bodies that work together to promote better working practices and better working relationships. Here's a rundown of the standards relating to business continuity management.

Standard	Comments
AS/NZ HB 167: Security Risk Management (2006) Developed by: Standards Australia Country: Australia	HB 167 is a security risk management framework that outlines a broad framework and core processes for inclusion in a security risk management process, project, or program of work. It is consistent with the framework for risk management outlined in AS/NZS 4360 (2004): Risk Management. Security risk management (SRM) plays a critical role as part of an organization's risk management process in providing a fundamental assessment, control, and treatment process for certain types of risks. Applies to any size or type of organization that needs to develop security risk management processes.
AS/NZ HB 221: Business Continuity Management (2004) Developed by: Standards Australia Country: Australia	HB 221 is a voluntary standard that provides consistency in respect to business continuity and risk management. This standard states that the key outcome of the business continuity management process should be to identify what the minimum level of acceptable performance is and what infrastructure and resources are required to achieve and sustain it. HB 221 applies to any size or type of organization that needs to develop business continuity management processes.
AS HB 292: A Practitioners Guide to Business Continuity Management (2006) Developed by: Standards Australia Country: Australia	HB 292 is a guide that provides an overview of practices used within Australia, the United States, and the United Kingdom. The structure of the guide is based on HB 221:2004, with much of the information being fully consistent with HB 221. However, the principles of HB 221 have been significantly expanded upon and extensive new explanatory information is provided. Applies to any organization that needs effective business continuity management processes.
AS/NZS 5050: Business Continuity—Managing Disruption Related Risk (2009 Draft) Country: Australia	5050 builds upon Australia's HB 292 by contemplating a range of disruption risks that it integrates into risk management frameworks based on AS/NZS 4360 (2004) and AS/NZS/ISO 31000 (2009). 5050 enables businesses to protect cross-organizational functions and departmental structures. 5050 allows organizations to build flexible capability and cope with change and disruptive events.

(continued)

Standard	Comments
	5050 integrates with existing management system standards including: ISO 9001 (Quality Management Systems), ISO 27001 (Information Security Management), ISO 28000 (Supply Chain Security Management System), and ISO 14001 (Environmental Management Systems).
	5050 integrates into existing assurance processes without providing separate certification regimes or an additional compliance.
	The standard has three parts:
	1. 5050.1 Part 1: Specification
	2. 5050.2 Part 2: Practice
	3. 5050.3 Part 3: Assurance
	5050 applies to any organization that needs a business continuity management system (BCMS) or requires third-party certification of its approach to business continuity management.
ASIS SPC.1: Organizational Resilience: Security, Preparedness, and Continuity Management Systems (2009)	ASIS SPC.1 is a management framework that helps organizations manage and survive interruption events and take all appropriate actions to help ensure the organization's continued viability.
	ASIS SPC.1 provides a comprehensive approach for incidents resulting in an emergency, crisis, or disaster.
	It applies to any organization that requires business continuity management.
ASIS: A Practical Approach for Emergency Preparedness, Crisis Management, and Disaster Recovery (2005)	The ASIS guideline is a tool that considers the factors and steps necessary to prepare for interruption events.
	This is a voluntary guideline.
	The ASIS guideline applies to organizations interested in developing business continuity capabilities.
Bank of Japan: Business Continuity Planning at Financial Institutions (2003) Country: Japan	This is a mandatory standard for all Japanese financial organizations. It covers both mitigation of business interruption risks and continuity of critical activities.

(continued)

Standard	Comments
BASEL II: Revised International Capital Framework (2006)	BASEL outlines a set of principles that provides a framework for the effective management and supervision of operational risk for banks, including business continuity. These requirements are mandatory for a select number of banks based on asset size.
	Applies to internationally active banks at every tier within a banking group, any holding company that is the parent entity within a banking group, and banks that have capital recognized in capital adequacy measures and is readily available for depositors.
BCI: Good Practice Guidelines (2008)	The Business Continuity Institute (BCI) guidelines provide an approach that a practitioner can use to build or improve a business continuity program.
	BCI's Good Practices are voluntary guidelines for businesses, but mandatory for those individuals seeking professional certification from the BCI.
	Similar to the DRII Professional Practices, applies to any organization with a need for business continuity.
BS ISO/IEC 17799:2005 Code of practice for information security management Developed by: The British Standards Institution Country: United Kingdom	ISO/IEC 17799:2005 is a code of practice for information security, which includes business continuity within its scope. 17799:2005 establishes guidelines and general principles for initiating, implementing, maintaining, and improving information security management in an organization. The objectives provide general guidance on the commonly accepted goals of information security management. 17799:2005 contains best practices of control objectives and controls in the following areas of information security management: • Security policy • Organization of information security • Asset management • Human resources security • Physical and environmental security • Communications and operations management • Access control

(continued)

Standard	Comments
	• Information systems acquisition, development, and maintenance
	• Information security incident management
	• Business continuity management
	• Compliance
	The control objectives and controls in 17799:2005 are intended to be implemented to meet the requirements identified by a risk assessment. 17799:2005 is intended as a common basis and practical guideline for developing organizational security standards and effective security management practices and to help build confidence in interorganizational activities.
BS 25777: Information and Communications Technology Continuity Management (2008)	BS 25777 describes how to implement IT service continuity. Specifically, it helps organizations:
	• Plan and implement an information and communication technology strategy
	• Demonstrate they are prepared for an IT disaster
	• Show that they have an effective strategy to manage the loss of Internet, e-mail, or company information
	• Provide reassurance to business partners
	Applies to any organization that wishes to develop, implement, establish, and maintain a BCMS or requires third-party certification of its approach to business continuity management.
BS 25999 Business Continuity Management, Parts 1 & 2, The British Standards Institution.	BS 25999 is a voluntary standard that was built on the Business Continuity Institute's (BCI) earlier PAS 56. It is the most widely adopted standard and provides a credible route for certification. It provides end-to-end business continuity management framework and supporting management system.
Country: United Kingdom	BS 25999 applies to any organization that wishes to develop, implement, establish, and maintain a BCMS or requires third-party certification of its approach to business continuity management.

(continued)

Standard	Comments
Canada: Operational Security Standard—Business Continuity Planning (BCP) Program (2004) Country: Canada	This standard provides direction and guidance to Canadian government departments on setting up a business continuity management program that provides for the continued availability of: • Services and associated assets that are critical to the health, safety, security, or economic well-being of Canadians or the effective functioning of government • Other services and assets when identified by a threat or risk assessment The standard is supplemented by a set of technical documents that includes suggestions, examples, best practices, and other guidance.
CSA Z1600: Standard on Emergency Management and Business Continuity Programs (2008) Country: Canada	The CSA Z1600 is a voluntary standard based on the NFPA 1600. It has minor changes as a Canadian standard. CSA provides a benchmark to allow organizations to assess and then initiate their business continuity plans and strategies. Applies to Canadian government departments establishing their business continuity programs and is used in the private sector as a voluntary standard.
COBIT 5 (2012)	COBIT is a COSO-based IT governance framework. COBIT enables IT departments to align to the business objectives and determine the appropriate service and process models to support the business. COBIT deals with the creation, testing, and monitoring of a continuity and contingency plan. COBIT is a voluntary guideline that applies to the objectives and scope of IT governance, ensuring that its control framework is comprehensive, in alignment with enterprise governance principles, and, therefore, acceptable to boards, executive management, auditors, and regulators. COBIT controls can easily be expanded to provide greater cover for business continuity management.

(continued)

Standard	Comments
DRII: Ten Professional Practices (1999)	The Disaster Recovery Institute International (DRII) Professional Practices established the necessary skills and competencies for individuals focused on business continuity; more specifically, to establish requirements, define strategies, document plans, exercise strategies, and advance awareness among all stakeholders. The Professional Practices are voluntary guidelines, but mandatory for anyone applying for professional certification with DRII.
	Although focused on individual competencies, DRII 10 practices can be "retrofitted" to any organization.
FFIEC: Business Continuity Planning Booklet (2008)	The FFIEC is responsible for establishing standards to which financial institutions are held. The booklet outlines basic standards for business continuity management.
	The 2008 version included additional focus on:
	• The role of the board and senior management
	• Pandemic planning
	• Risk-management integration
	• Proactive risk mitigation
	• A general attempt to eliminate the ambiguity of earlier versions
	This is a mandatory regulatory requirement that applies to US banks and their service providers.
FFIEC: Interagency Statement on Pandemic Planning (2007) NOTE: Now included in the 2008 FFIEC Business Continuity Planning Booklet Country: United States	The statement is not mandatory but puts forward actions and strategies financial institutions should strongly consider when developing pandemic plans and strategies.
	Most US-based financial institutions should consider implementing the strategies to meet US regulatory expectations. Although not mandatory, US regulators are strong advocates of its use, so it would be prudent for any financial organization to include it within its thinking.
	Applies to US financial institutions and their service providers.
FSA CP142: Operational Risk Systems and Controls (2002) Country: United Kingdom	CP142 is a mandatory requirement for any UK-based financial services organization.
	CP142 sets out high-level controls that are designed to protect consumers and ensure market confidence.

(continued)

Standard	Comments
GLBA: Gramm-Leach-Bliley Act (1999) Country: United States	The GLBA is mandatory for any US financial that keeps customer data.
	It is intended to protect the personal financial information held by financial institutions about consumers. The act says that institutions should take measures to protect against destruction, loss, or damage to customer information due to potential environmental hazards such as fire and water damage or technological failures.
	It empowers federal agencies and the US states to administer and enforce its principles. This regulatory requirement is mandatory for applicable entities.
	GLBA applies to all US financial institutions, which include not only banks, securities firms, and insurance companies, but also companies providing many other types of financial products and services to consumers.
ISO 22301:2012: Societal Security—Business Continuity Management Systems (2012)	ISO 22301:2012 outlines requirements to "plan, establish, implement, operate, monitor, review, maintain and continually improve a documented management system to protect against, reduce the likelihood of occurrence, prepare for, respond to, and recover from disruptive incidents when they arise."
	The requirements specified in this standard are generic and meant to be applicable to organizations of all types.
ISO/IEC TR 18044: Information Technology Incident Management (2004)	ISO/IEC TR 18044 provides guidance on information security incident management.
	TR 18044 covers:
	• Benefits to be obtained from information security incident management approach
	• Examples of information security incidents
	• Possible causes of information security incidents
	• Description of the planning and documentation required to introduce a good structured information security incident management approach
	• Description of the information security incident management process
	TR 18044 is relevant to any organization interested in implementing an information security incident management process.

(continued)

Standard	Comments
ISO (PAS) 22399: Societal Security: Guidelines for Incident Preparedness and Operational Continuity Management (2007)	ISO 22399 is a publicly available specification (PAS) that describes an organization's response processes (crisis and incident management). This is a voluntary guideline. ISO 22399 applies to organizations seeking to create or improve crisis or incident management response processes.
ISO/IEC 24762: Guidelines for Information and Communications Technology Disaster Recovery Services (2008)	ISO 24762 is a voluntary standard focused on DR sites and service providers seeking evidence of disaster recovery ability, either internally or as a commercial offering. ISO 24762 applies to any organization with internal recovery sites or offering disaster recovery services.
ISO 27001/17999: Security Techniques for Information Security Systems (2005)	ISO 27001 is a voluntary standard that specifies the requirements for establishing, implementing, operating, monitoring, reviewing, maintaining, and improving a documented information security management system within the context of the organization's overall business risks. ISO 27001 can be used as the basis of certification in the development of an information security management system. IS 27001 is applicable to a wide variety of organizations that are interested in implementing an information security management system or benchmarking their capability.
ISO 28000: Specification for Security Management Systems for the Supply Chain (2007)	ISO 28000:2007 specifies a security management system, including those aspects critical to security assurance of the supply chain. Security management is linked to many other aspects of business management. Aspects include all activities controlled or influenced by organizations that impact supply chain security. These other aspects should be considered directly and where and when they have an impact on security management, including transporting these goods along the supply chain. ISO 28000 applies to organizations involved in manufacturing, services, storage, or transportation at any stage of the production or supply chain.

(continued)

Standard	Comments
NEN 7132: Security, Preparedness, and Continuity Management Systems (2008 Draft)	NEN 7132 provides: • Guidance on the management of audit programs • The conduct of internal or external audits of security, preparedness and continuity management systems (including incident management, crisis management, and disaster management) • Guidance on the assessment of auditors. NEN 7132 applies to many potential users, including (but not limited to) auditors, organizations implementing management systems, organizations needing to conduct audits for contractual reasons, and organizations involved in auditor certification or training.
NFPA 1600 Standard on Disaster/ Emergency Management and Business Continuity Programs Developed by: The National Fire Protection Association Country: United States	This is the established US standard for business continuity. It covers business continuity, emergency management, and incident management. NFPA 1600 has not been widely adopted, partly because it's not well known outside the United States.
NYSE Rule 446/NASD 3510/3520 (2004) Country: United States	Rule 446 requires that members establish and maintain business continuity strategies and plans relating to an emergency or significant business disruption. Rule 446 also requires that members' business continuity plans be designed to enable it to meet its existing obligations to customers. This regulatory requirement is mandatory for applicable entities. Applies to all members and member organization of the NYSE or NASD.
SEC 17 CFR 240 (2005) Country: United States	SEC regulations require that financial transaction histories be maintained for all electronic securities transactions and backup power be in place to maintain continuity. This regulatory requirement is mandatory for organizations operating within US securities broker–dealer industry.

(continued)

Standard	Comments
Singapore TR19: Technical Reference for Business Continuity Management (2005) Country: Singapore	TR19 is a voluntary standard that addresses the question of business continuity management and the recovery of critical processes. TR19 covers: • Preventive measures • Business continuity planning • Emergency response • Crisis communications • Supply chain coordination • Cooperation with industry and public authorities Applies to Singapore-based organizations that need business continuity guidance.
SS 540: Singapore Standard for Business Continuity Management (2008) Country: Singapore	SS 540 is a Singapore-based certifiable standard (that replaces TR19 (2004)). SS 540 establishes a framework for an organization to analyze and implement strategies, processes, and procedures. SS 540 emphasizes resilience and protection of critical assets including people, facilities, and other intangible and tangible assets. SS 540 is applicable to Singapore-based companies that desire to build resilience and an effective response to interruptions.
SS 507: Singapore Standard for Business Continuity/Disaster Recovery (BC/DR) Service Providers (2004) Country: Singapore	SS 507 provides a basis to certify and differentiate the BC/DR service providers. SS 507 helps organizations to select service providers and provides quality assurance. SS 507 also establishes industry best practices to mitigate outsourcing risks. SS 507 is applicable to BC/DR service providers who wish to get certified under the standard as well as BC/DR service providers or other organizations who can use the standard as a reference document.

(continued)

Standard	Comments
SI 24001: Security and Continuity Management Systems (2007)	SI 24001 is a framework that addresses emergency preparedness. SI 24001 incorporates risk and threat analysis as the basis for preparation of a management program.
	The standard is based on the assumption that a security event cannot be categorically prevented. Therefore, it contains a requirement to prepare plans for response and recovery in order to minimize the harm to the organization and its stakeholders.
	Applies to any organization that wishes to protect itself from the impact of a disruptive event.
White Paper on Strengthening the Resilience of US Financial System (2002)	Advises larger financial institutions on steps necessary to protect the financial system.
	The paper presents three new business continuity objectives:
	• Rapid recovery of critical operations following a wide-scale disruption
	• Rapid recovery following loss of staff
	• High level of confidence that internal and external continuity arrangements are effective
	The paper puts forward recommended objectives. However, the guidance is generally viewed as mandatory by the wider financial service industry in the United States.
	The paper targets all US institutions that are providing financial services, especially those deemed "critical" by the agencies. The requirements do not, however, apply to the recovery of trading operations or retail financial services.

Severity Levels

As mentioned in Chapter 1, if criticality levels provide a measure of how important something is to the business, severity levels tell us how significant events are. The following table is an example of severity levels. You may decide to list more or have different criteria or names. It's the principle that matters; the exact implementation is irrelevant as long as it's consistent within your organization and represents a sensible way of breaking incidents up.

Severity	Description
Critical	Significant risk to the continued operation of the whole enterprise
Severe	Significant risk to the continued operation of a business division or geographic region
Major	Risk to the continued operation of a major function, system, or key location
Significant	Risk to the continued operation of a secondary site, function, or system
Minor	Risk to the continued operation of a team, minor process, or system
Noncritical	Risk to noncritical activities, systems, or individuals

Mapping Severity Levels to Criticalities

As mentioned in Appendix K, if criticality levels provide a measure of how important something is to the business, severity levels tell us how significant events are. This table shows how the two interact. RTO, you will recall, stands for recovery time objective. Chapter 1 provides more on criticality and severity.

Severity	Criticality
Critical	0–2 which equates to an RTO <4 hours
Severe	0–2 which equates to an RTO <4 hours
Major	2–4 which equates to an RTO <24 hours
Significant	4–5 which equates to an RTO <48 hours
Minor	5–6 which equates to an RTO <1 week
Noncritical	7–8 which equates to an RTO >1 week

Index

Get the eBook for only $10!

> Now you can take the weightless companion with you anywhere, anytime. Your purchase of this book entitles you to 3 electronic versions for only $10.

This Apress title will prove so indispensible that you'll want to carry it with you everywhere, which is why we are offering the eBook in 3 formats for only $10 if you have already purchased the print book.

Convenient and fully searchable, the PDF version enables you to easily find and copy code—or perform examples by quickly toggling between instructions and   applications. The MOBI format is ideal for your Kindle, while the ePUB can be utilized on a variety of mobile devices.

Go to www.apress.com/promo/tendollars to purchase your companion eBook.

All Apress eBooks are subject to copyright. All rights are reserved by the Publisher, whether the whole or part of the material is concerned, specifically the rights of translation, reprinting, reuse of illustrations, recitation, broadcasting, reproduction on microfilms or in any other physical way, and transmission or information storage and retrieval, electronic adaptation, computer software, or by similar or dissimilar methodology now known or hereafter developed. Exempted from this legal reservation are brief excerpts in connection with reviews or scholarly analysis or material supplied specifically for the purpose of being entered and executed on a computer system, for exclusive use by the purchaser of the work. Duplication of this publication or parts thereof is permitted only under the provisions of the Copyright Law of the Publisher's location, in its current version, and permission for use must always be obtained from Springer. Permissions for use may be obtained through RightsLink at the Copyright Clearance Center. Violations are liable to prosecution under the respective Copyright Law.

Other Apress Business Titles You Will Find Useful

Metrics
Klubeck
978-1-4302-3726-6

CFO Techniques
Guzik
978-1-4302-3756-3

Using Technology to Sell
London
978-1-4302-3933-8

Exporting
Delaney
978-1-4302-5791-2

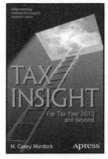

Tax Insight
Murdock
978-1-4302-6310-4

**How to Recruit and Hire
Great Software Engineers**
McCuller
978-1-4302-4917-7

**When to Hire—or Not
Hire—a Consultant**
Orr/Orr
978-1-4302-4734-0

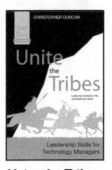

**Unite the Tribes,
2nd Edition**
Duncan
978-1-4302-5872-8

**The Handbook of
Financial Modeling**
Avon
978-1-4302-6205-3

Available at www.apress.com